HOT LEAD
ISSUE THREE

THE ADULT WESTERN SPECIAL

HOT LEAD
Issue Three
Published May 2019

Editor
Justin Marriott

Ghost editor and contributor
Paul Bishop

Contributors
Andreas Decker
Ian Millsted
Steve Myall
Tom Simon

Correspondence welcome
thepaperbackfanatic@sky.com

Copyright notice
All art reproduced for the purposes of historical context.
No copyright infringement intended.

HOT LEAD CONTENTS

The Adult Western Super Friends Page 4
Tom Simon on the Stan Lee of the adult western

The Sleazy Riders Page 6
Justin Marriott curates a visual guide which shows sex and westerns are as old as the hills

Sex and Six-Guns Page 12
Paul Bishop traces the development of the adult western genre

Bloodied Spurs Page 28
Justin Marriott gives a sprinkling of Cimarron

For a Few Issues More Page 32
Andreas Decker on the overseas exploits of Lassiter

The Trailsman Page 38
Steve Myall follows The Trailsman

Frontier Poet Page 42
Justin Marriott serves up Ruff Justice

Draw! A Top Ten of Western Comics Page 46
Ian Millsted provides a personal take on his Dirty Baker's Dozen from the world of comics

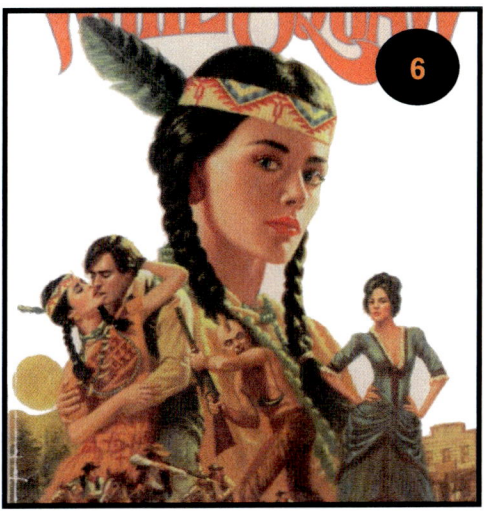

ADULT WESTERN SUPER FRIENDS

WHAT IF I TOLD YOU THAT THERE WAS A FOUR-BOOK SERIES THAT PUT MANY OF THE GREATEST ADULT WESTERN HEROES INTO ONE UNIVERSE WORKING TOGETHER TO VANQUISH EVIL FOES? ANYBODY INTERESTED IN AN ADULT WESTERN AVENGERS?

FEATURE BY TOM SIMON

Imagine a world where the following stars teamed up, interacted with one another, killed bad guys and got laid in a series of interrelated novels:

-Deputy U.S. Marshal Custis Long from the 'Longarm' series by Tabor Evans

-Jessie Starbuck and Ki from the 'Lone Star' series by Wesley Ellis

-The U.S. Cavalry soldiers from the 'Easy Company' series by John Wesley Howard

-Pinkerton agents 'Raider and Doc' from the series by J.D. Hardin

-Gunfighter John Fury from the 'Fury' series by Jim Austin

It's true. It happened in four books published in serial form between the years 2006 and 2009, and we have Stan Lee wannabe James Reasoner to thank for the creation of this audacious literary project.

There's no great roadmap anywhere explaining how to enjoy this historic confluence of horny violence, so let us be your guide.

You need to acquire the following novels all written by James Reasoner under the Tabor Evans house name. The reading order is important, so please pay attention as the

books aren't numbered on their covers:

- Longarm Giant 25: Longarm and the Outlaw Empress" (2006)
- Longarm Giant 26: Longarm and the Golden Eagle Shoot-Out" (2007)
- Longarm Giant 27. Longarm and the Valley of Skulls" (2008)
- Longarm Giant 28: Longarm and the Lone Star Trackdown" (2009)

Also bear in mind that 'Longarm' Giants were different than the standard 400+ book 'Longarm' adult western series. They were released annually, and each novel clocked in at about 300 pages whereas a normal 'Longarm' usually ran 185 pages. The Giants allowed the authors to write longer - and sometimes more complex - stories while allowing Jove Books to charge more for an Adult Western series paperback.

Each of the books listed above stars Custis Long, and the action generally ping-pongs between chapters told from the perspectives of the other adult western heroes participating in the books' adventures along with Longarm.

By way of background, it's important to know a little bit about the 'Lone Star' series before embarking on this 1200 page, multi-novel odyssey. The continuing story thread of the 'Lone Star' books dealt with a shadowy European crime cartel who killed Jessie Starbuck's father at the beginning of the series. Jessie and her Kung-Fu sidekick Ki have a bunch of mostly inessential adventures with bad guys being tangentially related to the cartel. Eventually, Jessie and Ki - with the help of Longarm - vanquish the cartel once and for all. But is the cartel really gone for good? As long as you understand the European cartel was bad and now is gone, you can now begin Longarm and the Outlaw Empress. The novels all do a nice job of reintroducing the co-stars, so you don't need to be intimately familiar with every series to enjoy this one.

There were other team-ups in the history of Adult Westerns. 'Edge' and 'Steele' met and joined forces. "Gunsmith #300" saw Clint Adams teaming up with Longarm with a cameo from Slocum (Fun Fact: All three heroes got laid, just not with one another). I believe 'The Trailsman' met up with Canyon O'Grady in at least one paperback.

However, nothing in the Adult Western genre has ever been as ambitious as Reasoner's project in these four 'Longarm' Giants. He did an amazing job with this story arc, and the books are individually and collectively fantastic. Seeing these characters interact with one another was a real pleasure and worth the investment of time and money to track these down. Highest recommendation.

We have Stan Lee - wannabe James Reasoner to thank for the creation of this audacious literary project.

THE SLEAZY RIDERS

A VISUAL GUIDE TO THE NOVELS AND MAGAZINES WHICH COMBINED WESTERNS AND SEX, EITHER SIDE OF THE RISE AND FALL OF THE 'ADULT WESTERN' PAPERBACK.

CURATED BY JUSTIN MARRIOTT

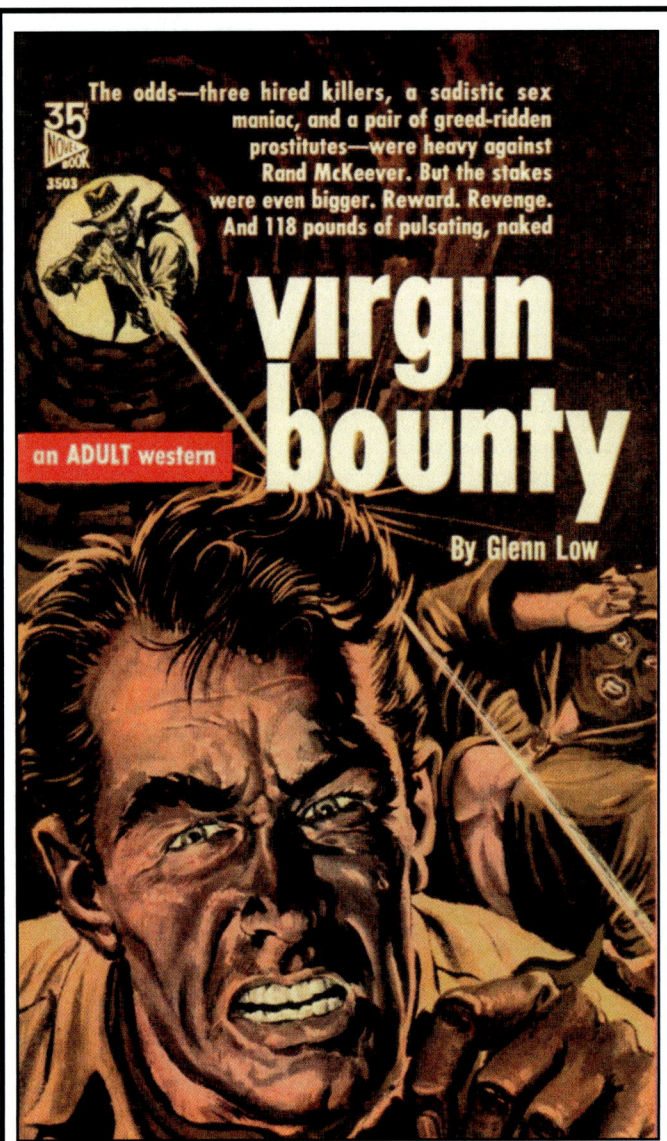

Pulsating and naked

Novel Books were a Chicago based publisher of girlie mags and sleaze paperbacks in the 1950's and 60's, with the latter now attracting a cult following due to their outrageous packaging, with testosterone fuelled hyperbole that often spoke directly to their readers. Anyone using the phrase "toxic masculinity" would have a cardiac if furnished with a fistful of Novel novels!

Robert 'Big Bob' Tralins, who authored a dozen or so two-fisted action-sleazers for Novel has gone into print to say they were Mafia-owned, which only adds to their mystique.

Pictured is one of their sleaze westerns from 1959, which is the first use I can trace of the phrase "adult western". Glenn Low was prolific for Novel, specialising in backwoods and hussies, as well as souped-up sexy westerns.

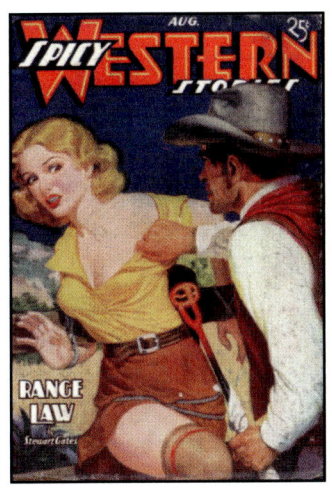

The Spice Girls

In the mid-30s, the 'Spicy' range of pulp magazines from the ironically named Culture Publications were hugely successful. Spicy being a code-word for Sexy at the time. **Spicy Western Stories** ran for the best part of 7 years.

The covers, most notably painted by H J Ward, followed a formula of a fair-skinned and blonde-haired female revealing her "alabaster bosom" as she wielded a six-gun or was menaced with a red-hot iron poker.

Each issue contained half-dozen shorts, with the focus on whip-lash quick action and lingering descriptions of the female form. Quaint by the standards of today, these were tamed by the authorities back in the day, and this title was renamed **Speed Western Stories**.

Innuendoes R Us

At the peak of the adult western, some publishers diversified into series with female characters in the lead. However, emancipation was rather lacking, as evidenced by the packaging of Zebra's **Head Hunter** and **White Squaw** series. Which carried titles such as *Rough Shaft*, *Desert Squeeze*, *Solid as a Rock*, *Badman's Climax*, *Desert Climax* and *Rough and Ready*.

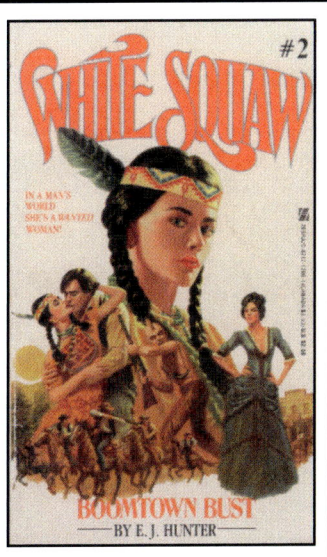

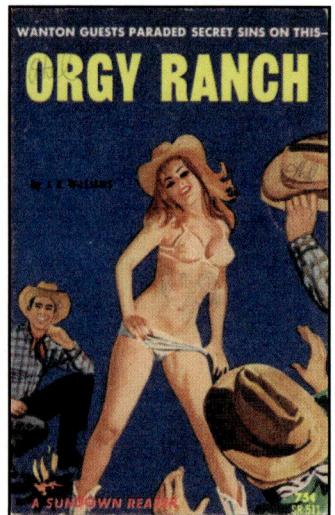

A fistful of Bonfils

The Greenleaf Imprints often made use of western motifs for their many sleaze titles, as can be seen by the gallery on the left. Robert Bonfils was the artist responsible for many of the more fun, colourful and energetic images that appeared on their covers. The stories were written conveyor-belt style, and based on my own experience, there are no western classics waited to be discovered in this canon.

However one title which is considered to be historically significant is *Song of the Loon* by Richard Amory, a 1966 account of a cowboy travelling across the American wilderness, taking in a number of homosexual encounters on the way, including native Americans. The Bonfils cover came with a blatant piece of phallic symbolism, something he was fond of sneaking into his paintings. The book was extremely successful, generating a sequel in the form of *Listen the Loon Sings*, a satirical version *Fruit of the Loon*, as well as a film adaptation.

Once upon a time in Hollywood.....

Ex-Hollywood actor Lynton Wright Brent was often credited as author at short-lived sleaze publishers in the latter half of the 60s. Brentwood (possibly his own imprint, combining his surname and Hollywood) put out the likes of *Silent Sex Trail* and *Lust Gallops into the Desert*. All read like reprints of standard oat-mealers book-ended with sex scenes added to fool horny browsers.

Sex and violence

In 1967 the sleaze publishers began to move from soft-core into hard-core, including the introduction of violence and non-consensual sex which can be seen in titles such as *Rawhide Killer*. The western-porn cross-over was generally rare, which based on this title is probably a good thing. Brandon House were known for the striking packaging of their books, as is evidenced by this particular cover.

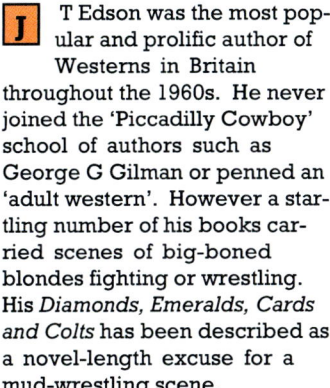

G.L.O.W.

JT Edson was the most popular and prolific author of Westerns in Britain throughout the 1960s. He never joined the 'Piccadilly Cowboy' school of authors such as George G Gilman or penned an 'adult western'. However a startling number of his books carried scenes of big-boned blondes fighting or wrestling. His *Diamonds, Emeralds, Cards and Colts* has been described as a novel-length excuse for a mud-wrestling scene.

South of the border

It can be argued that the spirit of the adult western lives on in the covers and pages of the Mexican comic-book **La Ley Del Revoler** (translated as **The Law of the Revolver**). Their outrageous machismo and sexuality has created something of a cult following amongst those interested in popular culture at the fringes. Very little information is available on-line that I can trace (a comics fanzine called **The Imp** published a special devoted to them and went bankrupt because so few sold!). But there are a number of examples of the original art available on-line, posted by various collectors, which I have reproduced across these pages. By all accounts, their contents are as outrageous as the covers suggest.

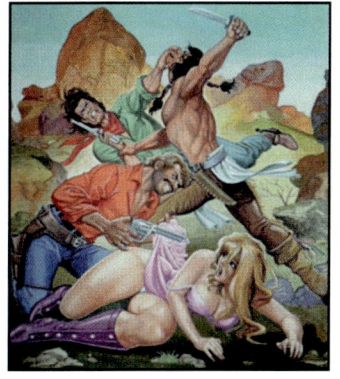

SEX AND SIX GUNS

THE ALL-AMERICAN ADULT WESTERN MAKES LIKE THE CAVALRY, SNATCHING THE WESTERN GENRE BACK FROM THE UPSTART BRITISH, WHILE ALSO USURPING THE WESTERN OF TRADITIONAL AMERICANA

FEATURE BY PAUL BISHOP

In the early '70s, a loose-knit group of British Western writers collectively known as The Piccadilly Cowboys (because none of them had been West of Piccadilly) turned the dying traditional Western genre on its head. Inspired by the cinematic style of the Spaghetti Westerns, the Piccadilly Cowboys spawned a series of ultra-violent Westerns—all of which owed allegiance to the iconic character, Edge, created by Terry Harknett (see Hot Lead Issue #1 for more).

For a decade, the Piccadilly Cowboys ruled the range with many different—yet ultimately similar—Western series. The British posse of wordslingers combined to produce over 300 novels. However, as the '80s dawned, the popularity of the Piccadilly Cowboy-style westerns began to wane.

Conventional Western wordslingers—who believed their vision of Western fiction had been dragged into the sewer by the British upstarts—began to breathe again. Clearly, the traditional Western of Americana would rise again from the ashes and return to the polite treatment of womenfolk, and clearly drawn lines between the white Stetsons and black Stetsons...

They couldn't have been more wrong...

The Piccadilly Cowboy Westerns were blood soaked, sadistic, jagged-edged tales containing enough gratuitous sex to shoot prudes to dollrags. In the void they left behind, a new generation of American pulp-style writers were a trigger-breath away from reclaiming the inherently homegrown Western genre for themselves.

This was not to be a return to the once beloved, but old-fashioned horse operas of staid-in-the-wool (yet

  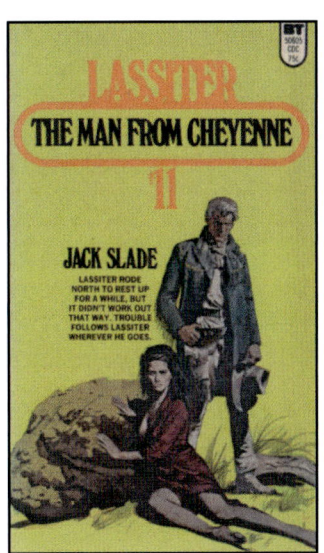

solid) storytellers like Louis L'Amour and Zane Gray. By mutating the genre into what would become known as Adult Westerns, this new generation of pulp wordslingers were ready to show the world anything the Brits could do, the Americans could do better and with a whole lot more sex. This was going to be a high noon showdown in the gutter—a hijacking at six-gunpoint of the paperback mass market.

The Piccadilly Cowboy Westerns placed their emphasis on violence first, with superfluous sex as an enticing afterthought. By comparison, Adult Westerns featured the hardcore sex front and center as the main reason for the books' existence.

Most of the Adult Western series rose to the same violence level of all but a few of the Piccadilly Cowboy series. But all of them provided the most blatant (rarely erotic) sexual copulations and fetishes to be found outside of brown paper covers. The likes of the upstanding Bonanza boys, Lucas McCain, and Matt Dillon had no idea what they were missing. Or if they did know, then their satisfying of the orgasmic needs of Wild West women was going on behind locked doors with the lights out...Say it ain't so, Marshal Dillon.

 ASSITER—There is an argument for considering the original Adult Western series being the Lassiter books, which first hit the spinner racks in 1968—eventually producing thirty titles. Produced by legendary low-end publisher Harry Shorten, the Lassiter series followed Shorten from Tower books, to Belmont Books, and finally to Shorten's last gasp company, Belmont—Tower.

Shorten wanted to get away from the traditional, upright hero cowboys portrayed in thousands of Westerns. He wanted the character of Lassiter to be the first American bred Western anti-hero. He imagined Lassiter as being more than a tough guy. He planned for Lassiter to be a complete bastard and an unrepentant son-of-a-bitch.

Shorten contracted Western regular W.T. Ballard to write the first four Lassiter books under the *house name* (a pseudonym most often owned by a publishing company to mask the identity of the many different wordslingers writing different series entries) Jack Slade. Shorten, however, was not happy

He imagined Lassiter as being more than a tough guy. He planned for Lassiter to be a complete bastard and an unrepentant son-of-a-bitch.

These were not to be nudge-nudge-wink-wink escapades over in a paragraph or two. These were to be explicit sex scenes running to several pages of graphic action unlike anything the Western genre had seen before.

with the results. Ballard could not shake the traditional characteristics of the Western heroes that were part of his writing DNA.

Ballard's Lassiter was a Robin Hood, a sort of Saint-of-the-West, still respectful of women and with a swear-less vocabulary. Even though Ballard had outlined a fifth book in the series, Shorten rejected it, determined to find a way to capture the character of his original vision.

Shorten turned to a young writer, Ben Haas, whose first novel had impressed him. Along with many other books, Haas would go on to create Fargo, one of the most iconic Western heroes of all time, under the name John Benteen. The Lassiter book Haas turned in to Shorten, *A Hell Of A Way To Die*, was much closer to the type of book Shorten wanted.

When Haas moved on to other projects, Shorten turned to his long time editor, Peter McCurtin—who would become a legend within the paperback original men's adventure genre. Taking over the reins of the series with book six, *High Lonesome*, McCurtain immediately proved he instinctively knew what Lassiter was meant to be.

McCurtin turned Lassiter into a dirty, bad-tempered, callous gutter fighter. In this new Lassiter's world, you shoot first (even from behind), punch below the belt (hard), swear (a lot), and rob, cheat, swindle, or kill anybody who gets in the way of the pursuit of large amounts of cash.

This rendering of Lassiter met Shorten's highest expectations—as well as the approval of readers. However, while the Lassiter series certainly contained a higher level of sexual content than was normal for the time of their publication, the books were not marketed as Adult Westerns.

Like the hard-hitting series from the Piccadilly Cowboys, the vio-

lence factor in the Lassiter books was still the main draw. The Lassiter series took a big step in the Western's mature evolution, but it was a precursor to the Adult Western—not the real sex oriented deal.

LOCUM—In 1975, Playboy Press began publishing the adventures of John Slocum, a drifting gunfighter and occasional Wild West outlaw. Written under the house name Jake Logan, Slocum was the first paperback original series to have the designation *'An Adult Western'* slapped prominently on the front cover. It was an immediate hit.

The origins of the Slocum series are murky and lost to time. The series concept was most likely the brainchild of Playboy Press editor Robert Gleason, who would shepherd it through the growing pains of the series' early entries.

For the first two books, Gleason concurrently commissioned writers Howard Pehrson and Rafael Hayes (other writers may have been commissioned at the same time to build up a series inventory). Why these two specific writers got the call is impossible to say, as they were not obvious choices. Perhaps one or the other or both had prior contact with Gleason, or were simply in the right place at the right time.

Aside from violent Western shoot-'em-up action, Gleason's bible for the Slocum series (a short synopsis given to the writers detailing the character and the series requirements) insisted on at least three hardcore sex scenes to appear somewhere in 60,000 words, which would make up the 198 page books.

These were not to be nudge-nudge-wink-wink escapades over in a paragraph or two. These were to be explicit sex scenes running to several pages of graphic action unlike anything the Western genre had seen before. Gleason made it

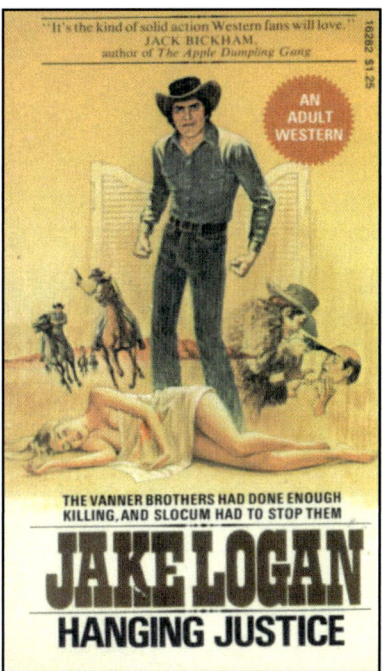

clear—the action, plot, and anything else in the book were secondary to the sex scenes. Even the main character's last name was an obscene pun if broken down into two words.

Disparate sources, many of them traditionally reliable, are inconsistent in their numbering of the Slocum books. Both *Ride, Slocum, Ride* and *Hanging Justice* are each listed as the first book in the series as often was they are each listed as the second book in the series. One source actually lists *Ride, Slocum, Ride* as #33 in the series—a confusion cause due to mistaken numberings during later reissues.

> **Even the main character's last name was an obscene pun, if broken down into two words.**

A closer look shows both books were published simultaneously. However, like twins being born seconds apart, one had to be the first. The inventory identifier numbers used by Playboy Press, which appear vertically in the top right-hand corner of the covers, clearly pinpoints the true order. *Ride, Slocum, Ride* comes in at #16281, while *Hanging Justice* is #16282—making *Ride* officially the first book in the series.

Under the pseudonym David King, Howard Pehrson wrote several war novels and westerns, but is best known for his six original *Rat Patrol* TV tie-in novels (which are now considered collectible—especially the sixth, *Desert Masquerade*). These were far longer and more intelligently written than many TV tie-in novels, which were often ground out by hack writers for a quick buck.

In *Ride, Slocum, Ride*, Pehrson pits Slocum against a repeatedly double crossing vixen who is out to take his gold. However, instead of the scar covered vicious gunfighter—who can shoot with one hand while throwing a knife with the other—as depicted on the cover, readers regrettably felt Slocum came across as *the most gullible weakling in the west*. Not a rousing endorsement to use as a cover blurb.

Rafael Hayes was a successful screenwriter with numerous television credits, including many for well-known Western TV series. His only novel outside the Slocum series was 1979's *Adventuring*—a big scale prairie horse opera.

Hayes' Slocum entry, *Hanging Justice*, sends Slocum in pursuit of the murderous Vanner brothers. Again, the book received complaints about the disjointed nature of the writing and the portrayal of Slocum as slightly insane.

Apparently, this critical battering had no effect on sales. The very large, but silent majority of readers (almost all male) were happy reading about Slocum getting his rocks off on a regular basis and didn't give a damn about the niceties of characterization, plot, or prose.

The books were successful enough for other writers to be brought into the Slocum fold. Some of these wordslingers, like Martin Cruz Smith, Jack Bickham, and others, would go on to become big sellers under their own names.

BUCKSKIN—By 1980, the Adult Western genre had become so successful most of the major paperback houses, including Jove, Berkeley, Pinnacle, and the notorious Zebra, had entries in the field. For a decade, new Adult Western series appeared and disappeared with the regularity of saddle sores on a tenderfoot.

Some series naturally lasted longer than others. In 1984, Leisure Books began publishing the Buckskin series which ran for 42 regular titles and 10 Giant titles. Giants were a marketing device to provide series readers with an occasional double length adventure of their favorite Western lothario.

Originally featuring *the adventures of Buckskin Frank Leslie, a cowboy whose talent with a gun is only surpassed by his way with the ladies*, book six finds Buckskin Frank Leslie dying and his son, Lee Morgan, is introduced and takes centre stage. From book #7 all the *Buckskin* books are about Lee Morgan.

Buckskin was created by Mitchell Smith—who wrote the first twelve titles under the pseudonym Roy LeBeau. The remainder of the series was published under the house name Kit Dalton, with most if not all entries being ghost written by Chet Cunningham.

PUR—At the same time, Leisure premiered Spur, which would become another popular Adult Western series running for 45 regular ti-

By 1980, the Adult Western genre had become so successful most of the major paperback houses, including Jove, Berkeley, Pinnacle, and the notorious Zebra, had entries in the field.

tles and 10 Giants. Spur was created and written exclusively by Chet Cunningham using the pseudonym Dirk Fletcher. The character of Spur McCoy was one of the wittiest and most clever adult Western characters. He was still a stereotype of the manly man, but less so than other Adult Western satyrs.

The one thing all these series had in common was a specific and directed editorial edict regarding the graphic sexual content. Having broken into the professional writing world myself via the Adult Western series *Diamondback* (I wrote #6 *Shroud of Vengeance* in the 9 book series), I received these blunt directions from the series editor first hand, *You can write whatever you want as long as there are two graphic sex scenes somewhere in the manuscript...*

THE TRAILSMAN—The bible written by an unknown editor for The Trailsman, another long running Adult Western series, takes a slightly softer approach...

The Trailsman novels are adult westerns of approximately 60,000 words, and as such have at least two sex scenes per book. The styles of these scenes have a wide range, but think of them as somewhere between romance and pornography, skirting the edges of explicit detail. Anatomical descriptions are somewhat veiled (i.e. "manhood" or "rod", but never "dick" or "penis"), but the action is always "hot". Flowery prose should be avoided, but neither should it be too blunt.

For 398 regular series entries and 7 Giant editions, The Trailsman—aka: Skye Fargo—had to put up with being a slightly more blushing hero than many of his harder-core counter-parts.

Signet Books began publication of The Trailsman in 1980 under the house pseudonym Jon Sharpe. The series was created by John Joseph Messmann. Best known as Jon Messmann, he was also the creator of another popular Adult Western series, Canyon O'Grady, as well as the men's adventure series Jefferson Boone: The Handyman. Exceedingly prolific, he was also one of the many contributing authors to the Nick Carter spy series.

Messman wrote most of the first 100 Trailsman books before retiring in the late 90s—even pairing up Skye Fargo and Canyon O'Grady in The Trailsman #87, *Brothel Bullets*. While authors such as Robert Randisi, Bill Crider, Ed Gorman, Will C. Knott, James Reasoner, and others (including some female authors) contributed one or more entries in the series, inexhaustible wordslinger David Robbins (best known in the Western genre for his Wilderness series) wrote almost all of the other Trailsman books.

BY THE NUMBERS—Despite the Slocum cash cow, after 38 series entries, Playboy Press went defunct. However, Slocum had become too popular to be allowed to fade away into pulp oblivion. The series was sold to Berkley in 1983, and was immediately turned into a monthly publishing juggernaut.

As was common with most paperback original series of the day, Berkley began by numbering each Slocum entry on the front cover—something Playboy Press had never done. But in a traditional effort by publishers to drive collectors crazy, instead of picking up the numbering consecutively after Playboy Press' 38th entry (*Law Comes to Cold Rain*) with #39, Berkley jumped ahead, labeling their first series entry (*Slocum's Cattle Drive*) as #50. Naturally, the gap of 11 phantom novels complicated the order of the books exponentially.

To confound collectors efforts further, when Berkley began reissuing the Slocum novels originally published by Playboy Press, they retroactively added numbers to the

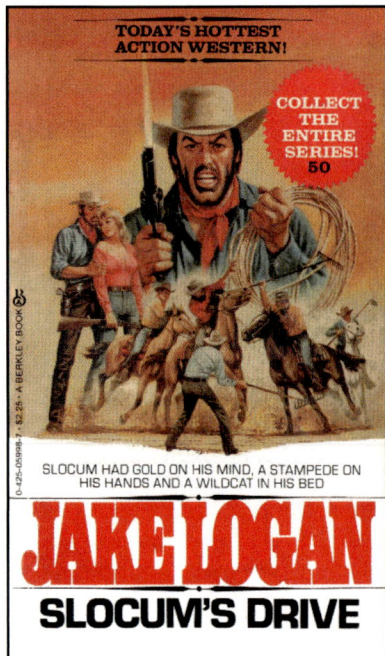

Berkley began by numbering each Slocum entry on the front cover—something Playboy Press had never done.

covers (starting with #1 *Ride, Slocum, Ride*). This didn't help as some of the titles were reprinted out of order. When further reprints were published over the coming years, the numbers on the front covers almost seemed randomly assigned (hence *Ride, Slocum, Ride* being reprinted as #33).

The Spur series also had numbering issues, as did many others. The first three Spur books had already been released when, for unknown reasons, the publisher decided to relaunched the series. In doing so, the publisher began the series from #1 again, but used completely new titles and stories, as if the original three books never existed.

Other publishers, such as Signet, were not above changing titles when the books were reissued. The Trailsman #1: *Seven Wagons West* has been listed on various Internet sources as The Trailsman #1: *Seven Ways To Die* (although, Western series experts have never run across an actual Trailsman book with this title). However, changing titles is another practice despised by series completists.

The happy-go-lucky approach to the numbering and titling of series entries really only bothered anal-retentive collectors. The average Adult Western reader (once compared derogatorily to mouth breathers in bars) didn't care what number was on the front cover as long as the number of graphic sex scenes burning up the pages inside remained high.

 EX IN THE SAGEBRUSH—The Slocum books were so successful, they continued to be published monthly until #430 *Slocum's Silver Burden*, which hit bookstore shelves (by this time drugstore spinner racks were a thing of the past) in November 2014. Subtracting the 11 phantom Slocum books from the 430 total, times 3 sex scenes per book, and you come up with a total of 1,257 sex scenes. Poor old Slocum must have been plum worn out.

For several years, Slocum could lay claim to being the longest running Adult Western series, before a couple of his Adult Western contemporaries broke his record, including one last holdout which is still being published today. There were several other Adult Westerns with similar long runs ending only slightly behind the mark set by Slocum. There were also a handful more with series runs of 100 plus. And there were a virtually uncountable number of Adult Western series with 50 entries or less.

 ONGARM—Lou Cameron was a sometimes inspired always solid

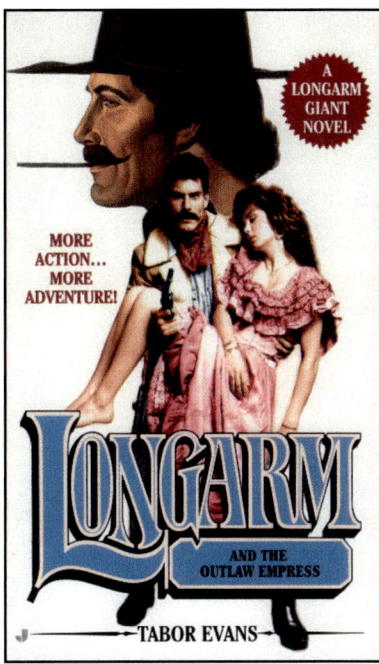

The covers of the Longarm novels all depicted the profile of Longarm's lived-in face graced with a mustache to make any '80s male porn star proud.

journeyman writer. In 1978, he was more than inspired when he created Deputy U.S. Marshal Custis Long, known to friends, enemies, and uncountable ladies across the West as Longarm. If you understandably thought Longarm was a cool nickname for a U.S. Marshal, as in *Long Arm of the Law*, you would be wrong. Jove Books wanted an Adult Western series to compete for the Slocum audience, so it doesn't take much lewd imagination to figure out what part of the male anatomy aroused the nickname.

Longarm is described as being a *lean, muscular Giant with the body of a young athlete and a lived-in face*. The covers of the Longarm novels all depicted the profile of Longarm's *lived-in face* graced with a mustache to make any '80s male porn star proud.

Lou Cameron wrote close to fifty entries over the course of the series under the publishing house's pseudonym Tabor Evans. Over the thirty seven years of Longarm's publishing history, many other authors also assumed the pseudo-

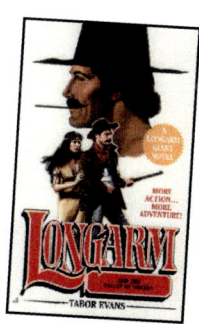

nym. Some were lesser known wordslingers beginning their writing careers. However, the vast majority of the authors were experienced and well-known wordslingers, including Will C. Knott, Frank Roderus, Chet Cunningham, J. Lee Butts, Gary McCarthy, James Reasoner, Jeffrey M. Wallmann, Peter Brandvold, and the legendary King of the Paperbacks—Harry Whittington.

Aside from the monthly series entries, there were also 29 Longarm Giant editions. The Longarm Giants were published annually and were not numbered on the covers as were the regular Longarm series books. However, the brilliant (but not always infallible) Fantastic Fiction website claims Jove jumped directly from Longarm Giant #10 (*Longarm and the Lone Star Captive*) to Longarm Giant #12 (*Longarm and the San Joaquin War*), making Longarm Giant #11 a phantom novel (not existing in any traditionally published format).

However, in discussing this with Western series maven Steve Myall, the assumption that the eleventh

Longarm Giant is a phantom does not appear to make sense. The tenth Longarm Giant, *Longarm and the Lone Star Captive*, was published in 1991, with *Longarm and the San Joaquin War* being published a year later in 1992, in keeping with the annual schedule, which would make it the eleventh Longarm Giant, not the twelfth.

What is more likely is the two year gap between the sixteenth Longarm Giant, *Longarm and the Lusty Lady*, published in 1996, and the next Longarm Giant, *Longarm and the Calgary Kid*, published in 1998, with the missing Longarm Giant year being 1997—making the non-existent (and unnumbered) Longarm Giant #17. All of this is (ridiculous) speculation, but definitely the type of finite detail fanatical collectors (not me, honest, not me...) love to chew over, and over, and over.

While the average Longarm tale ran approximately 185 pages, the Longarm Giants hit the 300 page range. This not only allowed the writer of the Giant edition to write a more complex story line, but it also allowed Jove to charge significantly more money for entries in their most popular Adult Western series.

Longarm would run until 2015 when it abruptly ended with Longarm #436: *Longarm and the Model Prisoner*. Every one of the series entries provided a stable concoction of what their audience wanted—prurient sex, bullets flying from blazing six-guns, vicious fist fights, more sex, more gunfights, and more sex. Longarm always got his man, and he always got more women than any man had a right to get.

THE CURSE OF THE COMPLETIST—Many of the same authors who wrote Longarm novels were also writing for other Adult Western series. The most prolific also added pseudonymous entries in the equally similar profusion of men's adventure series being concurrently published by the same publishing houses.

This created another interesting conundrum for collectors. The aforementioned legendary King of the Paperbacks Harry Whittington is popular enough with those in the know to make his six Longarm titles (#28 *Longarm On the Humboldt*, #32 *Longarm and the Golden Lady*, #35 *Longarm and the Blue Norther*, #40 *Longarm in Silver City*, #44 *Longarm in Boulder Canyon*, and #48 *Longarm in the Big Thicket*—all published between '81 and '82) among the most collectible in the series.

However, there are a number of unidentified author attributions in not only the Longarm saga, but in many of the other Adult Western series. Trying to pin down who wrote what in the world of Adult Westerns and Men's Adventure paperback original series has become an obsessive pastime for collectors trying to accumulate full runs of a specific author's works.

While Lawrence Block and Donald Westlake didn't write Adult Westerns or Men's Adventure series entries (or did they?), their almost uncountable early soft-core sex novels, written under who knows how many pseudonyms (some known, some not), are highly sought after hot items for their acolytes—who keep discovering titles even forgotten by their authors.

Some mega-selling writers would prefer to have their sordid past in Adult Westerns and Men's Adventure series never come to light. After the success of *Gorky Park*, Martin Cruz Smith was outed for many of his pseudonymous paperback original series novels. He originally tried to distance himself from what he considered blots on his record, even refusing to sign copies of those books when presented with them by fans. He has grumpily rescinded this hardline

> **Trying to pin down who wrote what in the world of Adult Westerns and Men's Adventure paperback original series has become an obsessive pastime for collectors trying to accumulate full runs of a specific author's works.**

stance, but don't catch him on a bad day.

 ONE STAR—Jove not only used the Longarm Giants to further the adventures of their bestselling Adult Western character, but also to introduce fans to the gunslinging, and breathtakingly beautiful heiress, Jessie Starbuck (capable of *shooting like a man, loving like a woman*) and her murderous protector, the Kung-Fu kicking Ki. Using the popularity of Longarm to throw support behind the launch of Jessie and Ki's own Adult western series, Lone Star, was smart marketing on the part of Jove.

Starting in 1982 with the first Longarm Giant (*Longarm and the Lone Star Legend*), Jessie and Ki continued to team-up with 'ol Custis Longarm in each of the first ten Longarm Giants (right up to the missing Longarm Giant #11—somebody somewhere has to know the story behind the skipped number).

Within a month of Jessie and Ki's Longarm Giant debut, the first Lone Star novel made a big splash on the bookshelves. It was packaged exactly as the Longarm series, with similar cover art, interior design, and a similar number of hot sex scenes. Using the Jove owned pseudonym Wesley Ellis, Western novel stalwart Jeffrey M. Wallman was tapped to pen Lone Star #1 *On the Treachery Trail*.

Many of the regular scribes for the Longarm series contributed stories to the Lone Star saga. Jeffrey M. Wallman, who wrote Lone Star #1, contributed many other entries, as did Neal Barrett, Jr.

Lone Star was notable for a number of reasons. First it featured what has since become a familiar theme mixing Western tropes with the Kung-fu action made popular by the films of Bruce lee and the *Kung-Fu* television series starring David Carradine.

Second Lone Star featured a strong female lead character, which inevitably introduced cunnilingus into the pages of Adult Westerns. Not sure what male readers made of this new diversion. However, it didn't matter if they were amused, appreciative, or appalled, it certainly didn't hurt sales.

Lone Star quickly established an interesting and versatile story line. To begin the series, Jessie Starbuck's father is murdered by a secret European crime cartel. Jessie and the Kung-Fu kicking Ki's adventures were often connected, at least tangentially, to her quest for revenge against the cartel. It's important to note that with the help of Longarm, Jessie and Ki are eventually able to destroy the cartel and bring the storyline to an end—or did it?

Lone Star ran until 1995 with the final book in the series being #153 *Mountain of Fire* (there were no Lone Star stand-alone giants as all of Jessie and Ki's appearances in Giant editions were team-ups with Longarm and labeled as Longarm Giants). In 2006, however, Jessie and Ki would return to ride again in Longarm Giant #24 *Longarm and the Undercover Mountie*. Proving more than versatile, their future held more team-ups with Longarm.

In 2006, the ever reliable and amazingly prolific wordslinger James Reasoner began an exceptional four book Longarm Giant story arc. As mentioned earlier, there had been Adult Western character team-ups before (The Trailsman and Canyon O'Grady, The Gunsmith and Longarm, Edge and Steele), but usually—not always—these involved characters from series within the same publishing house, and usually created by the same author. But Reasoner took this concept to a whole new, never before considered level.

Starting with Longarm Giant #25 *Longarm and the Outlaw Empress* and continuing through Longarm Giant #25 *Longarm and the Outlaw Empress*, Longarm Giant #26 *Longarm and the Golden Eagle Shoot-Out*, Longarm Giant #27 *Longarm and the Valley of Skulls*, and wrapping up in Longarm Giant #28: *Longarm and the Lone Star Trackdown*, Reasoner pulled out all the team-up stops. It was as if he was assembling an Adult Western version of Marvel's superhero team-ups.

Pitting Longarm against a new crime cartel—rising from the ashes of the cartel he assisted Jessie Starbuck and Ki to defeat—forms the framework for the quartet. Obviously, Jessie and Ki were involved in the action along with The U.S. Cavalry soldiers from Easy Company series (written under the house name John Wesley Howard), popular Pinkerton agents Raider and Doc (whose adventures were recounted under the pseudonym J.D. Hardin), and gunslinger John Fury (the lead series character written under the pseudonym Jim Austin). The narrative shifted between each of the characters and back as the story unfolded.

Between 2006 and 2009, Reasoner did a spectacular job of maintaining both quality and continuity over the course of the four books. Using broad strokes, he quickly introduced characters to readers who might

---

Packaged similarly to the other Adult Western series including the style of the cover art, The Gunsmith was an immediate success.

---

be unfamiliar with them, while never letting the backstories interfere with the crackling six-gun action.

These four book form the magnum-opus of the Adult Western genre. An accomplishment, I doubt we will ever see the likes of again. Because of the seamless manner in which they were written, perhaps the most overlooked aspect of the quartet is each novel can be read as a standalone tale, while all four also tie together as one continuous Adult Western version of *War and Peace*.

As a last note on the Lone Star series, Jessie and Ki would team-up with Longarm one final time in Longarm Giant #29 *Longarm and the Railroad War*. And finally, in 2012, a Longarm/Lone Star Omnibus, entitled *Sweet Revenge*, was published. It comprise the first Longarm Giant (*Longarm and the Lone Star Legend*—in which Jessie and Ki made their debut) attributed to Tabor Evans, and Lone Star #1 *On the Treachery Trail* attributed to Wesley Ellis.

HE GUNSMITH—With 439 regular series entries (and counting) alongside 16 Giants, The Gunsmith created by Robert J. Randisi (writing as J.R. Roberts) now stands alone as the granddaddy and arguably best Adult Wester series. Starting in 1982 with The Gunsmith #1 *Macklin's Women*, the series has changed publishers, cover artists, and even formats a number of times, yet loyal fans of The Gun-

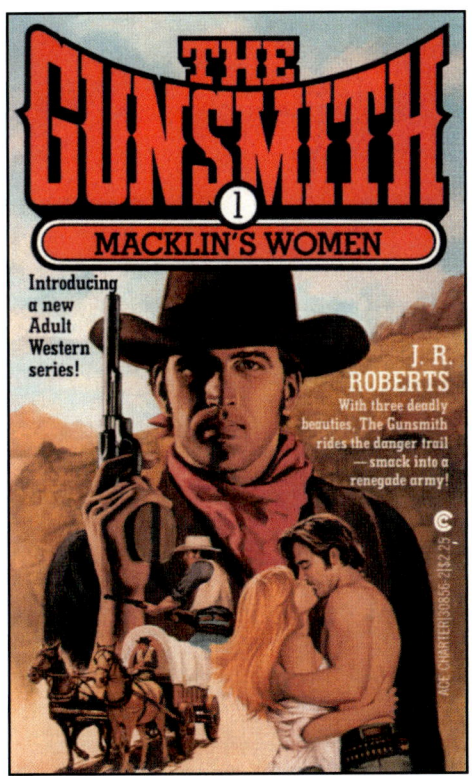

smith have followed their hero every step of the way.

The Gunsmith is ex-lawman Clint Adams. With the badge behind him, Adams travels the West as an itinerant gun trader and gunsmith. He also regularly finds beautiful and willing women along the way who can't wait for him to lie with them in bed, on a saddle blanket, in a hayloft, or anywhere else coitus can be achieved.

Randisi has been called *the last of the pulp writers*. However, while there are still a few others around and a new generation behind them, Randisi has proven to be one of the most prolific and resilient of writers having written close to six hundred books.

Commercially, The Gunsmith is unique in that it is owned not by a publisher, but by Randisi himself. Furthermore, all but a rare few of the 455 regular/giant series entries have been written by Randisi (during one switch to a new publisher, the series editor commissioned several Gunsmith books from other writers to establish a backlog).

The Gunsmith was created shortly after Slocum appeared from Playboy Press along with the debut of Longarm from Jove Books. The success of the first two Adult Westerns prompted an editor from Charter Books to approach Randisi and ask if he could write Westerns with sex in them. Randisi immediately agreed, although he had never written a Western—with or without sex. Packaged similarly to the other Adult Western series including the style of the cover art, The Gunsmith was an immediate success.

While turning out monthly novels featuring The Gunsmith, Randisi would also find time to create and write other Adult Western series. Including Tracker (as Tom Cutter—7 books), and Angel Eyes (as W. B. Longley—9 books). Both series deserved longer runs.

In 2017, using his J. R. Roberts pseudonym, Randisi began writing a spin-off from The Gunsmith series—Lady Gunsmith. Published by Speaking Volumes (also current publishers of The Gunsmith series), Lady Gunsmith is Roxanne Louise Doyle. Known as Roxy, Lady Gunsmith is the daughter of Gavin Doyle. When she was a child, traveling west on a wagon train, her mother was killed, leaving her father alone to raise and care for her. Unsure of himself in this endeavour he proceeded the only way he knew how, with a gun. He traveled, hiring out as a bounty hunter, and sending the money to a family in Missouri who were raising Roxy. Eventually, the money stopped coming, and the assumption was Gavin

Doyle was dead. Wanting confirmation, Roxy dons britches, boots and a man's work shirt, packs a dress and her foster father's big Navy Colt, and travels west, becoming the legend known as Lady Gunsmith along the way.

In the early 80's, Charter Books who were publishing The Gunsmith agreed to let Randisi start a Lady Gunsmith series. The idea fell by the wayside when Berkley bought The Gunsmith series from Charter. However, Randisi never lost the idea or the desire to write the character of Lady Gunsmith. In 2015, Randisi brought the idea up again with his agent over lunch in New Orleans. His agent mentioned the series to Speaking Volumes, who eagerly agreed to publish Lady Gunsmith 36 years after it was originally proposed to Charter Books.

Starting with Lady Gunsmith #1 *The Legend of Roxy Doyle* in 2017, the series has recently seen publication of Lady Gunsmith #5 *The Portrait of Gavin Doyle*. Apparently there is no end in sight for either The Gunsmith or Lady Gunsmith, and certainly no end to Randisi's prodigious talents.

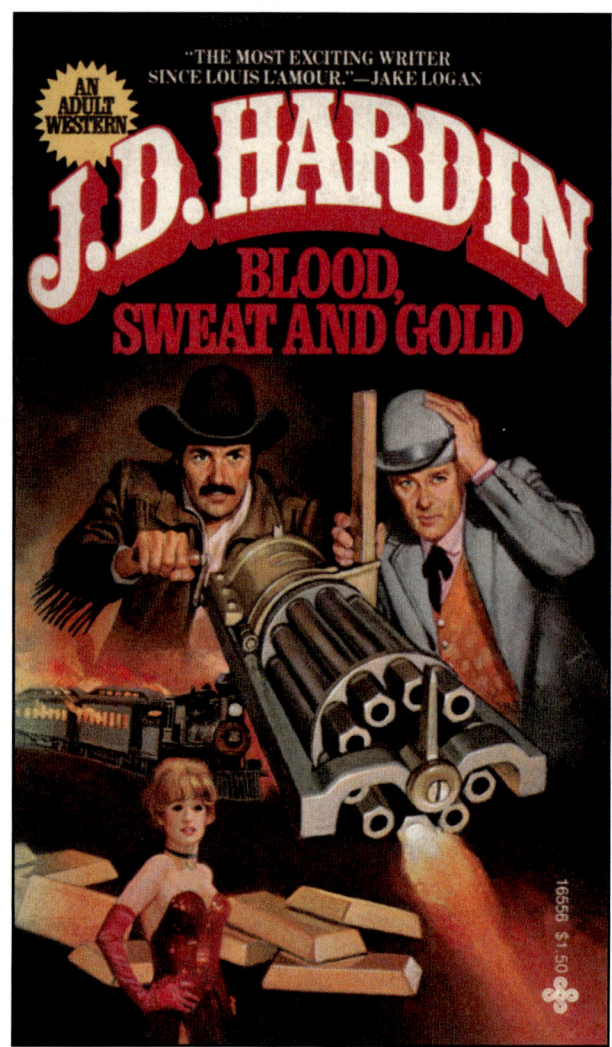

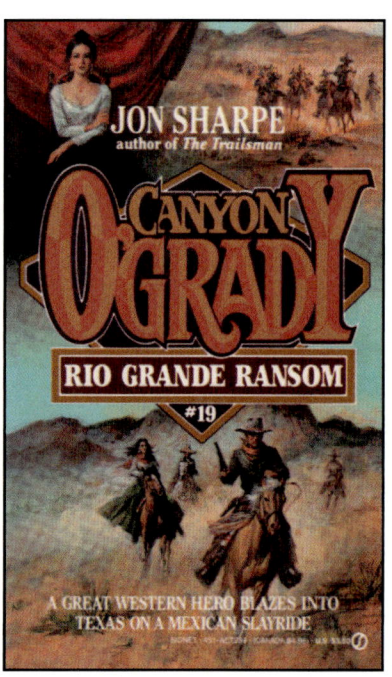

THE LIFE AND TIMES OF THE ADULT WESTERN—The one of the obvious social conceits of all these books is the message that sex on the frontier was free of such trivial considerations and complications as sexually transmitted diseases, pregnancy, impotence (these guys never, ever, wore out no matter the number of performances demanded), or relationship and commitment issues.

Giving a totally different interpretation of how the West was won, the life of an Adult Western hero was a Grand Guignol performance of fast horses, fast guns, and faster women. The hero's larger than life action exploits necessitated the combined nine lives of an overpopulated planet of cats, and an unending supply of nubile, busty, bawdy, heavily panting, oversexed, objectified females.

The failure of politically corrected history classes in school is exemplified by their removal of any mention of this from their textbooks. The Adult Western is to be lauded for providing us with an unvarnished picture of frontier life.

OTHER ADULT WESTERN SERIES OF NOTE

CANYON O'GRADY—Created by Jon Messmann (The Trailsman) and published by Signet, Canyon O'Grady was a an early prototype Secret Service Agent assigned to Washington, D.C. Often working at the behest of the president, O'Grady plied his trade more as a western detective, going undercover on occasion to break up criminal conspiracies. The series was written by Messmann, Chet Cunningham, and Robert Randisi. David Robbin's was offered The Canyon O'Grady series, but turned it down. As prolific as he was/is, Robbins felt he would have to give up writing the Trailsman series in order to take on the O'Grady books. He felt strongly about continuing to write about Skye Fargo (The Trailsman), which turned out to be the right choice.

There is an interesting editorial error in the early pages of Canyon O'Grady #4 *Shadow Guns* when O'Grady is misidentified as Sky Fargo, hero of The Trailsman series from the same publisher (and quite possibly the same writer).

DOC AND RAIDER / RAIDER—Doc and Raider was a popular Adult Western series written by the usual suspects along with Victor Milan, Neal Barrett Jr, and Donald Bain (known for his Murder She Wrote novels) under the house name J.D. Hardin. Beginning in 1979, with Doc and Raider #1 *Blood, Sweat and Gold*, the series ran until 1987, ending with Doc and Raider #73 *Hell On the Powder River*. Published by Berkley, the title characters are problem magnet Doc Wheatherbee (Doc), and his go to problem solver—a lusty Pinkerton agent (Raider) with a penchant for trouble and women. Many of the women who cause Doc problems turn out to be Raider's former lovers.

In an interesting marketing ploy, while ending the Doc and Raider series, Berkley immediately began publishing a companion series, featuring the solo adventures of Raider. Continuity to the first series was established with similar cover art and packaging, and retaining the J. D. Hardin pseudonym. Raider continued to operate as lone hero until 1990 when the series ended, appropriately, with Raider #42 *End of the Trail*.

RENEGADE—He is called Captain Gringo, but his real name is Richard Walker, a soldier-of-fortune in the Old West wanted by a variety of governments for his actions, and a variety of

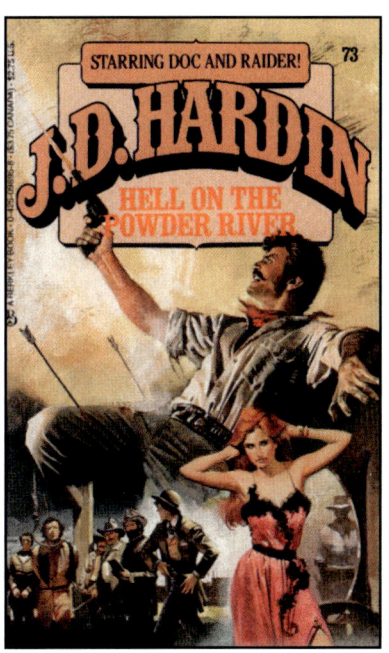

The Adult Western is to be lauded for providing us with an unvarnished picture of frontier life.

women for the same reason. From Renegade#1 *Renegade* in 1979, to Renegade #36 *Guns for Garcia* in 1986, the vigorous and virile Captain Gringo plied his fighting skills across Central and South America. Devised and written by Lou Cameron (creator of Longarm) under the pseudonym Ramsay Thorne, Renegade was a sort of X-rated version of John Benteen's iconic Fargo character. However, the sex in the Renegade series became seriously kinky with no fetish left unwhipped. Still, it was a well written and fun series, becoming a favorite Adult Western of many serious genre fans.

GUNN—The late Jory Sherman published more than 300 books. While freelancing novels in other Adult Western series, he ultimately joined the parade by creating his own Adult Western series, Gunn.

When William Gunnison is blamed for his wife's murder, he goes on the run. Hiding his identity as the deadly outlaw known as Gunn, he is out for vengeance against the real killers.

While the formula is familiar, Sherman is a master at plotting, writing amazing action scenes, and having an innate understanding of what his readers want. Beginning in 1980, with Gunn #1 *Dawn of Revenge*, and ending in 1987, with Gunn #29 *Mine Shaft*, Sherman produced arguably the best series in the Adult Western genre.

If you're keeping count, that's 29 books in 7 years—all excellent Western adventures, and all written by Sherman—surprisingly— under his own name. If you haven't read this series, grab your spurs and a fast horse and get to it.

CIMARRON—While writing a traditional western series (Luke Sutton) for Signet, Leo P. Kelley also jumped on the Adult Western bandwagon creating Cimarron, also published by Signet. Starting in 1983, with Cimarron #1 *The Hanging Judge*, Kelly wrote a total of 22 series entries, ending with Cimarron #22 *Hired Guns* in 1986.

He rode from Texas with his Colt at his side, his Winchester in a saddle scabbard, a look in his eyes that made men back off, and a lean, muscled strength that made women gaze at him long and hard. He called himself Cimarron, with his hand on his gun to answer any more questions. He alone knew of the one kill-crazy act that had cut his life in two, and turned him into a man without a home or a friend on either side of the law.

A little less bawdy than most Adult Westerns, Cimarron tried to walk a tightrope between traditional westerns and the sex heavy adventures pursued by Longarm and Slocum.

RUFF JUSTICE—The Ruff Justice Adult Western series, written by Paul Lederer under the pseudonym Warren T. Longtree, had no qualms about detailing the sexual frontier adventures of the titular character. Ruff Justice is a scout for the US Army, which gives him plenty of opportunities to bed not only pioneer women and cavalry wives, but also a number of hot Indian maidens. The series ran for 28 books between 1981 (Ruff Justice #1 *Sudden Thunder*) and 1986 (Ruff Justice #28 *The lady Was An Outlaw*).

ZEKE MASTERS—While mostly a run of the mill Adult Western, the Zeke Masters books are unique for having the series named after the author and not the main character, Faro Blake. In reality Zeke Masters was a pseudonym for Ron Goulart, a popular and prolific pulp, mystery, fantasy, and science fiction writer. Goulart wrote 31 westerns as Zeke Masters between 1980 (*The Big Gamble*) and 1983 (*Up For Grabs*).

ADULT WESTERN SERIES

Trying to catalogue every Adult Western series would be a chore of epic proportions. What follows is an extensive, but admittedly incomplete, list of Adult Western series and the author or pseudonym most closely associated with them...

Agent Brad Spear—Chet Cunningham
Angel Eyes—Robert Randisi
Angel Eyes—W.B. Longley
The Apache Wars Saga – Len Levinson
Ash Tallman—Tom Lord
Bear Haskell—Peter Brandvold
Blake, Faro—Zeke Masters
Blaze—Stephen Mertz
Bolt—Cort Martin
Breckenridge Saga—Chet Cunningham
Bronc—Jeffrey M. Wallman
Buckskin—Roy Labeau/Kit Dalton
Bushwhackers—B.J. Lanagan
Chance—Clay Tanner
Cimarron—Leo P. Kelley
Diamondback—Pike Bishop
Diamondback—Guy Brewer
Doc & raider—J.D. Hardin
Easy Company—John Wesley Howard
Faro Blake—Zeke Masters
Foxx—Zack Tyler
Golden Hawk—Will C. Knott
Gunn—Jory Sherman
Gunslick—J. G. White
Gunslinger—J.R. Samples
The Gunsmith—J.R. Roberts
The Hangman—Craig Foley
Hatch, Fancy—Zachary Hawkes
Head hunter— E.J. Hunter
Horne, T.G.—Pierce Mackenzie
Jim Steel—Chet Cunningham

Justice, Ruff—Warren T. Longtree
The Kansan—Robert E. Mills
Lady Gunsmith—J. R. Roberts
Lone Star—Wesley Ellis
Longarm—Tabor Evans
Long Rider—Clay Dawson
Mcmasters—Lee Morgan
Molly—Stephen Overholster
Mountain Jack Pike—Joseph Meek
O'Grady, Canyon—Jon Sharpe
Pecos Kid—Jack Bodine
Preacher's Law—Dean L. Mclwain
Quinn's Raiders—J.D.Bodine
Raider—J.R.Roberts
Ruff justice - Warren T. Longtree
Ryder—Cole Weston
Saddler—Gene Curry
Saddle Tramp—Clint Hawkins
The Scout—Buck Gentry
Searcher—Josh Edwards
Shelter—Paul Ledd
Slade—Link Pennington
Slater—Jackson Cain
Slocum—Jake Logan
Spur—Dirk Fletcher
Stringer—Lou Cameron
Texas tracker - Tom Calhoun
Tracker—Tom Cutter
The Trailsman—Jon Sharpe
White Squaw—E.J. Hunter
Wildgun—Jack Hanson

BLOODIED SPURS

DESPITE THE COVER PROMISE OF "ALL THE VIOLENCE AND THE PASSION OF THE OLD WEST", THE CIMARRON SERIES WAS SIGNIFICANTLY DIFFERENT TO THE OTHER ADULT WESTERN SERIES OF THAT ERA.

FEATURE BY JUSTIN MARRIOTT

The typical origin of a western series (anti-)hero of that time would focus on how his entire family were raped and murdered by a gang of blood-crazed cut-throats, and that despite being staked out and left to die by the criminals, our vengeful hero would survive and go on to hunt them down, dispatching each one with a bullet and a pun. Cimarron's origin and modus operandi are much less lurid, with him leaving home as a teenager to become a cattle-hand in order to escape the strict rules of his evangelist father rather than in the heat of a blood-soaked vendetta.

Something of an expert frontiersman, Cimarron is a success in his new career until he makes the mistake of contradicting his fool-hardy boss. Newly unemployed and drifting through the country-side, Cimarron has the misfortune to encounter a reverend and his daughter who aren't all they claim to be. Falsely accused of the

> **You certainly get the impression that Cimarron isn't the sharpest tool in the box, and his tendency to think with parts of his body other than his brain gets him into hot water on more than one occasion**

robbery and murders the counterfeit couple have committed, Cimarron finds himself face to face with Judge Parker who has a reputation for hanging first, asking questions later. Of course, Cimarron proves his innocence at the very last moment and finds new employ as Judge Parker's deputy sheriff, which acts as the spring-board for continuing entries to the series.

In addition to his rather low-key origin, Cimarron's physiology is different to many other western characters. You certainly get the impression that he isn't the sharpest tool in the box, and his tendency to think with parts of his body other than his brain gets him into hot water on more than one occasion. Something of a recurring joke in the series are scenes in which a naked Cimarron is in hot pursuit of a femme fatale who has utilised her feminine wiles to pull the wool over Cimarron's eyes. Although of course, Cimarron is prodigiously endowed and a real stud, so the formula isn't too subverted.

Cimarron also attempts to resolve conflict without violence, and when in physical confrontation resorts to his fists with gun-fire a last resort- a far more realistic way for the law to act than most westerns in which every saloon is one poker card turn away from a Peckinpah-on-steroids style shoot-out.

Author Leo P Kelley is the name credited with the majority of the Cimarron series, a name I would more readily associate with science fiction. Further inspection of Kelley's bibliography suggest he started as a SF writer in the 1960s, but by the late 1970s was diversifying into other genres including westerns where he also penned a Luke Short series. Three of the entries were credited to Lew P Baines, a pseudonym used by three authors, including Robert Randisi - a hugely prolific writer who at that time also contributed to other western series such as Angel Eyes, as well as several entries to The Destroyer

Gorgeous cinematic covers from Scottish-born artist Ken Barr, depicted Cimarron amongst a montage of scenes from each adventure

men's adventure series before eventually enjoying success in the crime genre.

I was initially attracted to the series by the gorgeous cinematic covers from Scottish-born artist Ken Barr, which depicted Cimarron amongst a montage of scenes from each adventure. Inevitably there would be the scar-faced hero in the embrace of some lusty wench, a lead-coated shoot-out and Cimarron menaced by a wild creature- wolves, vultures, red ants and a rabid possum (!) all taking their turn. That Barr illustrated all 22 covers using the same template makes this an attractive series to collect.

I noticed very little difference between the Kelley and Baines entries, which is to the credit of the authors and editors involved. I detected that Baines' efforts were harder-edged and more sexually explicit. Whereas Kelley excelled with brutal and gritty fist-fights which, while they consist of bone-crunching and nose-splitting well beyond the endurance of any normal man, carry an edge of excitement and authenticity. It's the air of believability that make this such an enjoyable series; whether the accounts of life as a cattle-man, or the types of crimes that Cimarron is sent to deal with, the books

The Cimarron series

1. Cimarron and the Hanging Judge, 1983
2. Cimarron Rides the Outlaw Trail, 1983
3. Cimarron and the Border Bandit, 1983
4. Cimarron in the Cherokee Strip, 1983
5. Cimarron and the Elk Soldiers, 1983
6. Cimarron and the Bounty Hunters, 1984
7. Cimarron and the High Rider, 1984
8. Cimarron in No Man's Land, 1984
9. Cimarron and the Vigilantes, 1984
10. Cimarron and the Medicine Wolves, 1984
11. Cimarron on Hell's Highway, 1984
12. Cimarron and the War Women, 1984
13. Cimarron and the Boot Leggers, 1985
14. Cimarron on the High Plains, 1985
15. Cimarron and the Prophet's People, 1985
16. Cimarron and the Scalp Hunters, 1985
17. Cimarron and the Comancheros, 1985
18. Cimarron and the Gunhawk's Gold, 1985
19. Cimarron on a Texas Man Hunt, 1986
20. Cimarron and the Earth People, 1986
21. Cimarron and the Manhunters, 1986
22. Cimarron and the Hired Guns, 1986

During Cimarron's origin there is no mention made of his facial scar which is clear on Ken Barr's cover depictions.

provide a believable insight to life on the frontier relative to its cousins.

One interesting anomaly occurs in book four, which reeks of editorial interference and an attempt to fit Cimarron in with the blood-and-soil extremes of the other "adult westerns". As Cimarron travels across the plains he decides to drop in on an old girlfriend who reveals he is the father of her son. Just as Cimarron decides to settle down with his discovered family, some pesky desperado drops by and shoots mother and son, in brain-splattering detail. Cimarron responds by staking out the killer with a razor-sharp spear underneath him and just enough slack in his restraints to allow him to arch his back away from the point. Until exhaustion sets in and he'll no longer be able to hold his back from sinking onto the spear....

This uncharacteristically sadistic scene is thrown in as a couple of chapters in the middle of the book and never referred to again. Possibly due to editorial requirements for a tougher approach, or reflecting that five different authors contributed to the series. It's also interesting that during Cimarron's origin in book one there is no mention made of his facial scar which is clear on Ken Barr's cover depictions. Again, I suspect someone at Signet asked the hero be roughened up, and Cimarron's origin was hastily expanded upon in book two to include the scar.

Possibly fans of the more explicit adult western series might find his adventures somewhat vanilla, but if you are looking for a gritty and more grounded series of 80s westerns, then I would recommend Cimarron.

FOR A FEW ISSUES MORE

THE STORY OF HOW WESTERN CHARACTER LASSITER EMIGRATED TO GERMANY WHERE HE ENJOYED A LENGTHY CAREER IN THAT COUNTRY'S 'HERTROMAN' DIGESTS.

FEATURE BY ANDREAS DECKER

Things went well for Bastei-Lübbe Publishing at the beginning of the 1970s. The publisher was a pillar of the Heftroman market. Its weekly crime pulp "G-Man Jerry Cotton", which had started in 1954, had become a brand name, if not a synonym for crime pulps available at newsstands. "Jerry Cotton" had three weekly editions - a new novel and two reprints - and a monthly paperback. It had even spawned a movie series from 1965 on. Bastei also had a large offering of other Heftromane in all genres, some aimed squarely at the woman's market, some at the men's market. Also, they did a lot of original comics for kids.

They also published westerns. In 1970 they had among others two long-running weekly western pulps. Bastei-Wildwest-Roman (1957-1997) and Bastei-Wildwest-Roman-Sonderausgabe (Special Edition) which later was renamed into Western-Hit (1961-1999). These were the usual anthology series popular in Germany at the time, every week a new self-contained novel, mostly written by German writers with American sounding pseudonyms like King Colt or Lex Lane. But change was in the air, the success of more violent western movies like the Peckinpah movies or the Spaghetti western had whet the appetite of the audience. So Bastei tried something different.

It bought the foreign rights for "Lassiter".

In 1968, Harry Shorten of the American outfit Tower Books wanted a new kind of Western hero – the anti-hero. And Lassiter was born. While in a traditional western the hero might be a Wells Fargo detective and the villain a bank robber, here it is the opposite. Lassiter is a man wronged and ruined by Wells Fargo, so he hits back the vigilante way. His nemesis is Sidney Blood, a detective of Wells Fargo. The first four novels were written by Willis Todhunter Ballard. But Shorten still wanted an even more ruthless kind of hero, less Robin Hood, more Man with No Name. Book six *High Lonesome* was written by Peter McCurtin, which was more to Shorten's liking. This Lassiter was a mean bastard, who did everything to achieve his goals while having sex with all the beautiful woman crossing his trail.

It was a kind of bold move for Bastei. Too much violence, sex and antisocial behaviour was a problem for the Heftroman market in Germany.

In Germany "Lassiter" debuted in 1970 as a paperback line. "Lassiter – Amerikas Grosser Western-Erfolg" (America's Big Western Success) the cover boldly proclaimed, while the back-cover of the first number told the prospective buyers:

"Do you want to commit suicide? No problem. Mess with Lassiter, and he will just pull the trigger. You don't need to insult Lassiter to die. Lassiter has killed many men for less. Lassiter wasn't born without mercy – but he learned fast. To be fair, he isn't more evil as his time or the men he kills. Lassiter doesn't dwell on all the men he killed, as he never killed someone who didn't deserve it – more or less."

It was a kind of bold move for Bastei. Too much violence, sex and antisocial behaviour was a problem for the Heftroman market in Germany. Entertainment material available by minors was and is monitored by the authorities, back then called Federal Review Board for Media Harmful to Minors (BPjS). If a product is deemed not suitable for minors after legal procedure, the authorities can enforce a ban which, among other measures, prohibits the sale and the advertising to minors. For a prod-

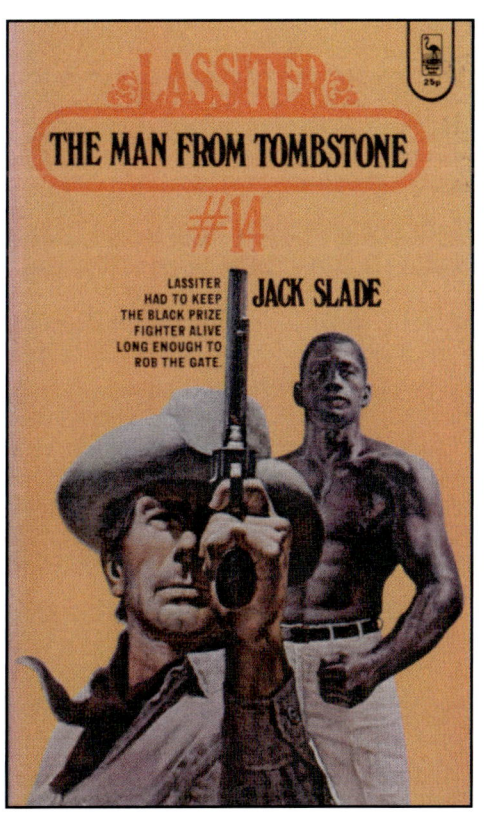

uct sold exclusively at every newsstand (and not an Adult Shop for instance which is closed to underage customers) this was a severe problem, resulting mostly in cancellation. Bastei seldom had problems with this board, "Jerry Cotton" was a model student in this regard. So, in some regards this new western was a bit playing with fire. Now paperbacks had a bit more leeway than the Heftroman, as they were much more expensive and mostly bought by older customers. Still, the editors couldn't have been happy when the novels went for even more violence and moral ambiguity with its hero. So, the translations had to be sanitized, a line cut here and there. The violence was toned down, but the sex scenes – tame as they still were in 1969 – were more or less untouched.

Also, it became pretty obvious that the Americans couldn't deliver enough material for a regular monthly paperback. In 1970 Tower only published three new novels, and Bastei's readership was accustomed to a punctual monthly release. A quarterly line couldn't be sustained at newsstands, where unsold books were sent back to the publisher after the new ones arrived. So Bastei also bought the rights for the character "Lassiter" and the house name "Jack Slade". Then it put its house writers on the job. No.11 was the first original novel written by a German writer.

To uphold the illusion that this was an exclusively American series, the editors went so far to invent fake title for the German books, the start of a tradition which in later years fooled many bibliographers. We will later come to that again.

"Lassiter" sold very well. Compared to the more traditional stuff like the Bastei-Western, another monthly paperback line, which did translations of writers like Louis L'Amour or Frank Gruber side by side with German originals, it had more bite. Indeed, it sold so well that Bastei only two years later introduced the series to the weekly Heftroman market. Editorial gave the development of the project to Günther Bajog, a seasoned pro, who had already written a lot of Heftroman westerns for the publisher. And Bajog wasn't amused. "They send me one of the paperbacks", he later told in an interview. "Lassiter was a brutal bastard, who slept with a woman and killed her in the morning after discovering that she was the leader of the outlaw gang. So I said: I don't want to do this. A few days later editorial called and gave me green light to write this as I wanted." Bajog retooled Lassiter back to a kind of Robin Hood in the west, again hunted by Sidney Blood and Wells Fargo, a drifter, who always let Greedo shoot first, to mix genre-metaphor's. Maybe some readers wondered why Lassiter wasn't the mean bastard of the early paperbacks any longer, but it seems nobody complained.

Lassiter No.1 – "The hardest man of his time" as the subtitle boldly proclaimed on the cover - debuted on 17. July 1972. The Heftroman with his lengths of traditionally 64 double columned pages - which is comparable to the novella with its 25000 to 30000 words – was at first published bi-weekly. But it sold so well that it became a weekly with issue 16. The paperbacks had established titles in which the name of the hero was always featured, emphasising the brand name, just like in America with "Longarm" or "Slocum" some time later. The weeklies continued this, every week it was "Lassiter and …" In later years this became more flexible.

The tradition of the fake title also was continued for some years, even for the Heftromane where traditionally no one reads the fine print. So, of the couple of hundreds of Heftromane and paperbacks outfitted with English titles only the 22 original Tower paperbacks – not all of the 29 novels done by Tower made the cut – are translations. No wonder that bibliographers are confused.

The erotic element of scantily clad or nude ladies was added, until it became a fixture of the series.

Initially, cover art was from German artists like Günther König, who later did such exceptional work for Bastei's competition with his covers for "Ronco – The Outlaw". Other European artists contributed to the series, a lot of Spanish studios. Motifs were random western impressions at first, tough westerners with guns and horses, always in action poses. The erotic element in the form of scantily clad or nude ladies was added, until it became a fixture of the series. Art underwent an evolution like the content of the novels did.

In the first years Lassiter was the eternal but basically noble drifter, always on the run from either the law or Wells Fargo. Each novel was a self-contained adventure, except for the basic background of the hero there was no continuity. So each week Lassiter encounters another villain, rights some wrongs and gets the girl. But

the sex scenes were not in the least explicit, more titillating than anything else, at best short paragraphs with a lot of euphemisms. Every few weeks there was another confrontation with Sidney Blood, in which Lassiter always triumphs. The action was fast, the historical background was basically exchanged for a mythical west, an amalgam of a horse, a colt, a western town as seen in the movies, some owlhoots and a lot of macho men in a nebulous, never defined time frame somewhere between the American civil war and the advent of the new century.

Sales were good, sales were indeed so well that soon there was a weekly reprint line, later even a third weekly reprint. But in 1980 Lassiter finally got a problem he couldn't outshoot. The BPjS put one issue of the weekly and three of the paperbacks on the index for being too violent and/or the glorification of vigilantism, among other complaints. In the mid-seventies the whole Heftroman market had become increasingly under fire for its violence, while the same battle was waged in the cinemas. Movies like *Django* or *The Evil Dead* only got ratings after severe cuts. The success of the then new horror pulps put the spotlight on the Heftroman medium. After a few series had to be cancelled, the industry made noticeable efforts of self-censorship. Violent content was toned down, translations were even more sanitized. But thanks to a change in the political climate to more conservative values at the start of the new decade a lot of product suddenly was again in the crosshair.

In the case of "Lassiter" both the paperback and the weeklies were one step before cancellation. But editorial found a solution to save the profitable western. Starting with issue 397 *Lassiter and the Rebel Horde*, the character was re-invented. Practically overnight Lassiter became "The Man from Brigade Seven". Now he was a secret special agent working for "Brigade Seven", a mysterious and fictional secret service of the government in Washington. Gone was the feud with Wells Fargo, gone was the gunman only working for himself, gone was the vigilante. Now the hero was fighting for law and order, a kind of James Bond in a never-changing west, just without the gadgets.

The readers took the changes in stride. Obviously, there wasn't much protest, as the western-series galloped on. Issue 1000 came and went. Along the ride the franchise lost the paperback line in 1996. Sales went down after the western genre suffered as a whole, so it was cancelled after 282 novels. In the course of time the formula never changed, but some things evolved. While the violence never became too gory because of the aforementioned reasons, even when the standards changed over the time, the erotic element became more explicit. At the end of the 90s it finally reached the level of your average Adult Western like "Longarm" and his competitors with its minute descriptions of sexual

encounters. Accordingly, the cover art became more erotic, often the naked beauties were more in the foreground than the western elements.

"Lassiter's" kind of a mythic west unburdened by history (or reality) and the emphasis on sex-scenes is often scorned and ridiculed by fans of the traditional western. But for all the cliché writing and the often one-dimensional plots the novels are competently or even very well written. In the end it is a question of talent, like in all pulp. In the course of its 47 years of existence some of the contributors to the pseudonymous "Jack Slade" became known, and it isn't just a man's game as one would suspect. Among the nearly 50 divulged writers there are quite a few women who have contributed to "Lassiter". Sometimes for a long time. In the last couple of years editorial made an effort to include more western history, so Lassiter meets persons like Buffalo Bill or General Custer.

Considering the rather generic nature of the novels "Lassiter" proved to have as much stamina sales wise as the hero has on the page. At the end of the 80s the western-genre finally fell out of favour. One series was cancelled after the other. In its best times Bastei had ten weekly western series at the newsstands, some of them reprint lines but mostly new novels. The publisher also never shied away to try something different or exploit trends, like the short-lived "Kung Fu Western" (47 issues, 1975-1977), a blatant rip-off of the tv-series with David Carradine, or the "Mexiko-Western" (38 issues, 1986-1988), adventures south of the border. But the last long-term success again had some connection with "Lassiter".

"Jack Slade – The hottest westerns of the famous writer of Lassiter" started in 1999. At first a weekly Heftroman and now a bi-weekly, it is a series of stand-alone western novels with the same erotic elements like "Lassiter", written by the same writers. Nowadays Bastei has only one competitor on this market-segment, which basically has become a reprint machine. The only original western novels written and published commercially for the sale at newsstands today in Germany are "Lassiter" and "Jack Slade".

In 2010 "Lassiter" reached issue 2000, at the time of writing issue 2500 is in the works. There are still two weekly editions, one original novel and one reprint line. Also, there is the E-book edition with often censored covers for the nipple-phobic online sellers. How long this will go on is anybody's guess. As witnessed in America the end can be quick; in the home of the genre the western has become as good as extinct as a market category. The Adult Western even vanished overnight. But in Germany "Lassiter" may yet ride on for a few years, bringing six-gun justice and seducing beautiful women every week.

A special thanks to Lynn Munroe and his indispensable research on Lassiter and to the writers of Zauberspiegel-online.de for their exhaustive work on the western Heftroman.

THE TRAILSMAN

RIDE ALONG WITH THE SERIES THAT PROMISED "THE SENSATIONAL, ACTION-PACKED SERIES WITH ALL THE VIOLENCE AND PASSION OF THE OLD WEST"

FEATURE BY STEVE MYALL

When my age was still measured in single figures, I was given a hardback book published by The Children's Press called The Rimfire Riders. It starred a man called Catsfoot who wore buckskins, was a scout, an expert tracker and lightning fast with his guns. I enjoyed the book so much that I soon owned the other two books featuring Catsfoot. I read these three books many times over and was always disappointed there weren't more.

Jump forward a number of years and during a trip to America I picked up four books in a series called The Trailsman. It's hero, Skye Fargo wore buckskins, was a guide, scout, expert tracker and lightning fast with his guns. All but in name here was my boyhood hero born again but there was a major difference; Fargo liked the ladies and they liked him a lot and their dalliances were described in explicit detail. I had discovered a new take on my childhood hero, here was Catsfoot for grown-ups and I set out on a quest to own all the books.

The Trailsman series was created by Jon Messmann and published by Signet under

the pseudonym of Jon Sharpe. The first two books hit the shelves in July 1980. Book three appeared in August and the fourth book in December. For a short-time the books were published roughly every three months, then two before becoming monthly publications from February 1983 and this continued until December 2014 when the series finally ended with book 398. Yes, if you do the maths the number of books doesn't add up to the number of years and that's because there were two books published in October 1999. There were also seven giant editions.

When the Trailsman was first launched it was marketed as an adult western series. This type of western was becoming very popular and added a much-needed boost to the sales of westerns and many such series were launched around this time. One of the reasons I liked The Trailsman so much, other than the reasons mentioned in my opening paragraphs, was the time it was set in, just before the American Civil War making

It was set in the time just before the American Civil War, making it stand out from the majority of the other adult western series as most were set in the 1880s.

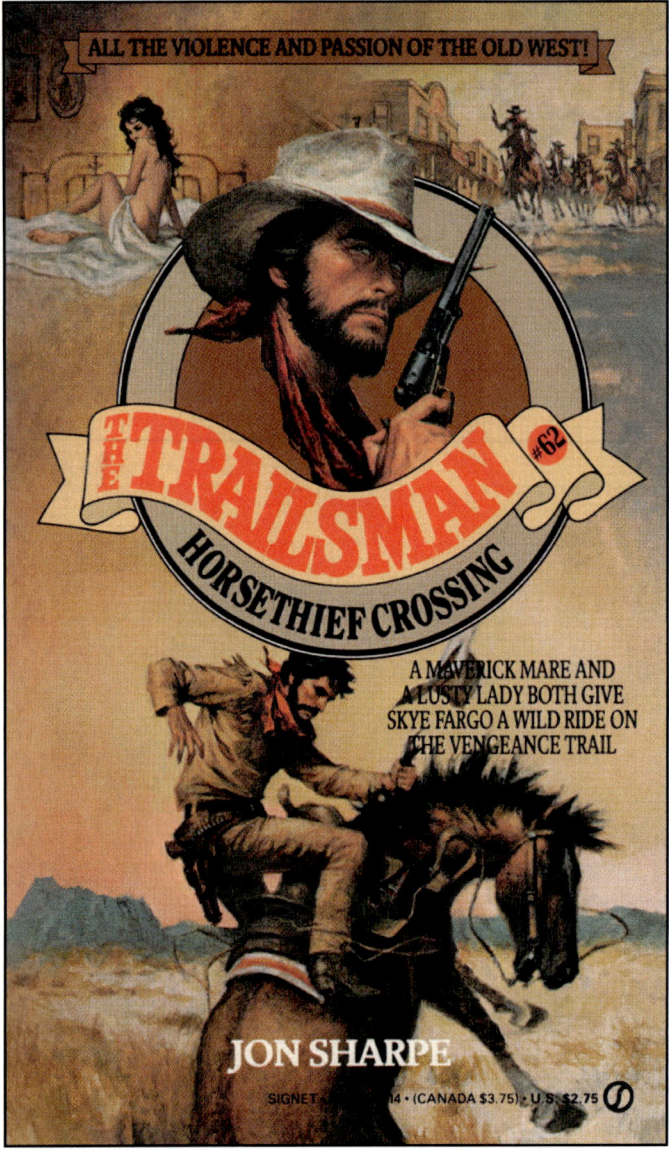

it stand out from the majority of the other adult western series as most were set in the 1880's.

Who was The Trailsman? Each book started with the following passages:

'Beginnings...they bend the tree and they mark the man. Skye Fargo was born when he was eighteen. Terror was his midwife, vengeance his first cry. Killing spawned Skye Fargo, ruthless, cold-blooded murder. Out of the acrid smoke of gunpowder still hanging in the air, he rose, cried out a promise never forgotten.

The Trailsman they began to call him all across the West: searcher, scout, hunter, the man who could see where others only looked, his skills for hire but not his soul, the man who lived each day to the fullest, yet trailed each tomorrow. Skye Fargo, the Trailsman, and the seeker who could take the wildness of a land and the wanting of a woman and make them his own.'

The adult content, graphic sex, was the major selling point when the series was launched and those early books contained a lot of it. The amount of sexual content wouldn't have been the sole reason this series lasted so long though, the overall quality of the storylines and writing would help to ensure its longevity and after a few years the number of sexual encounters, like in the other long-running adult western series, was reduced to around two per book and sometimes dealt with in a couple of paragraphs rather than pages as it was in those early books.

Other changes happened over the years, such as Fargo's mount being referred to as the Ovaro rather than a pinto. Many early books never mentioned Fargo being dressed in buckskins either. Fargo carries a Colt and an Arkansas Toothpick and for a long time used a Sharps but this latter weapon was eventually replaced with a Henry. Fargo's hunt for vengeance also faded into the background as the series progressed, although he does catch and kill one of those he is hunting in one of the early books but I don't think he ever caught up to the others. Some of Fargo's background can be found in book 6: *Dakota Wild* as the author fills the reader in on quite a bit of Fargo's history.

The Trailsman books are fast paced, action packed reads filled with twists and turns.

The Trailsman books are fast paced, action packed reads filled with twists and turns. Each book is a self-contained tale so a new reader to the series can jump in anywhere as there aren't any continuing storylines. Having said that there are a few characters that turn up in more than one book such as soldiers Fargo works for. One author even introduced a reoccurring sidekick, Snowshoe Hendee, that first appeared in one of said authors other series; **Dan'l Boone: The Lost Wilderness Tales** (books 8 and 11 to be exact). Another character that first appeared in book 87: *Brothel Bullets* and then again in book 100: *Riverboat Gold* is Canyon O'Grady who starred in his own 25 book series also published under the pseudonym of Jon Sharpe.

So who was Jon Sharpe? As already mentioned, Jon Messmann was the original author and creator of the series and virtually all the early books were written by him. It wasn't long before other writers joined the fold and a particularly strong period for me was when the writing duties were shared by Messmann, J.B. Keller and David Robbins. Robbins joined the team with book 118: Arizona Slaughter which came out in October 1991 and stayed with the series until its very end, having written more titles than any other author, in fact during the final couple of years was writing roughly eight of each year's books prompting James Reasoner to say, 'even though he (Robbins) didn't create the character, his version of Skye Fargo was the definitive one.' Another particular strong run for me was when Reasoner and Peter Brandvold wrote alongside Robbins.

Other authors who wrote as Jon Sharpe include James Wycoff, Barry Fremont, Jeffery Wallman, Ed and Martha Quillen, Frank Roderus, Will C. Knott, Glen Bavousett, Gary Goldstein, Robert Randisi, Alice Duncan, Steve Mertz, Ellen Recknor, Robert Vardeman, Ed Gorman, Fred Bean and John Edward Ames. Sadly, some of these authors didn't research the character of Skye Fargo well enough and got certain elements wrong but if you can ignore that fact their stories are still entertaining reads.

It's not only the writers who changed, the packaging did too. The cover style transformed eight times over the years. For me once the first look was altered, the wagon wheel background painted by Ken Barr, to covers showing more than one scene they got a lot better. In fact, I liked that each image depicted something that happened in the story unlike many of the competitor series that started using interchangeable characters that where cut and pasted into different compositions. Ken Barr was replaced by Jerome Podwil who singularly produced the artwork for a while before Hiram Richardson began painting the covers too. Both these artists staying with the series until Signet brought it to a close.

FRONTIER POET

RUFF JUSTICE WAS A QUIRKY SERIES PUBLISHED BY SIGNET, COMBINING A HERO CUT FROM A DIFFERENT CLOTH WITH TIGHTLY WRITTEN AND ACTION-FOCUSSED PLOTS.

FEATURE BY JUSTIN MARRIOTT

Paul Lederer (1946-2016), adopting the ludicrous pseudonym of Warren T Longtree, wrote all 28 Ruff Justice episodes from late 81-86. Something of a mysterious figure, Lederer typically refused to talk about his life, other than to suggest it had been a difficult one until he settled in California and carved out a successful niche writing series westerns.

He produced hundreds of books, his pseudonyms including Paul Ledd, Logan Winters, John Wesley Edwards and Owen G Irons. Lederer dismissed his westerns as hack-work, but there's no doubting that he was a professional writer in the finest sense of the expression. His Ruff Justice series are eminently readable saddle-operas, with a quirky lead character and unusual settings that fire the imagination.

Ruffin Justice debuted in *Sudden Thunder* (1981), which despite the standard "adult western" sex scene to open the book, soon detours into unusual territory when the

> **Justice dreams of a meadow full of blood-swollen flowers, through which he rides naked on a headless horse, before plunging into a river of flames from which he can't be rescued.**

spent Justice dreams of a meadow full of blood-swollen flowers, through which he rides naked on a headless horse, before plunging into a river of flames from which he can't be rescued. Some heavy symbolism and surreal imagery for what is work-for-hire in a cliché-bound genre. The following morning, Lederer describes Justice through the eyes of his bed-partner, as having fine, long dark hair, a torso patterned with scars and wearing an elk-skin outfit intricately patterned with beads.

Even quirkier than his appearance is Justice's propensity to write and perform his own love sonnets, which I guess passes the time when he is out on the range. And was probably author Lederer's personal challenge to help with his own interest in the assignment. Justice also owns a dog named Dooley, who runs beside Justice's horse when not indulging in the same pleasures as his owner (thankfully off-page!). Dooley seems universally disliked by readers, as he didn't appear in any further episodes, which I think is a shame. Maybe Dooley was by name and nature, rather genteel for an adult western series, but I think the idea of an anti-hero backed up by a flesh-and-blood weapon in the form of a ferocious dog or wolf is an interesting one. Only me? Oh well.....

Justice is employed by the US Cavalry for dangerous scouting missions, and in Sudden Thunder, that mission is to escort the grieving Denton family as they journey across Arizona to recover their father's body, killed whilst serving in the Cavalry. However, winter is coming in making the conditions dan-

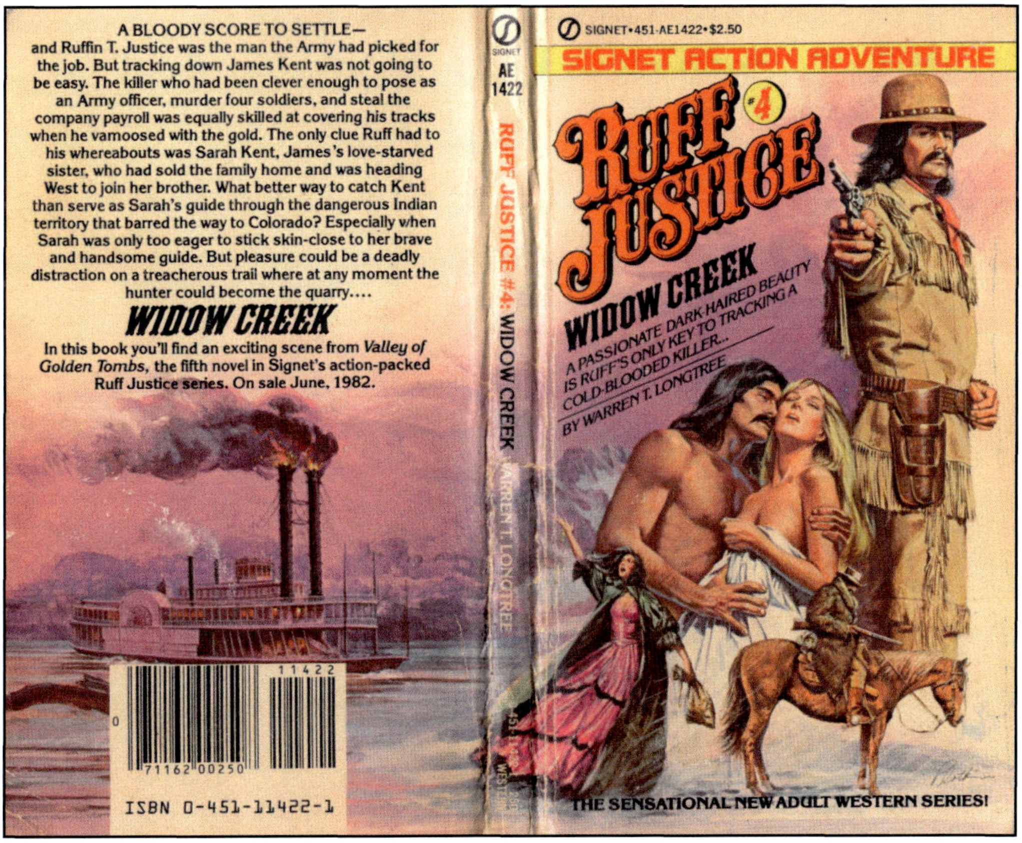

The Riverboat Queen utilised the unusual western setting of a steamboat. And added pirates!

gerous as they travel across river and mountain, and the local Sioux tribe are hostile to travellers. As their perilous journey unfolds, it becomes clearer that the Dentons aren't all that they claim, and the beautiful yet catatonic girl confined to their wagon is the key to unlocking the mystery behind the deception.

Sudden Thunder is a classic piece of series writing, with a small cast, a degree of tension set by their conflicting agendas, an increasing sense of drama due to these dynamics, all played out with author Lederer keeping the story-telling super-tight with an economic style of prose. With a plot device that could be applied to pretty much any genre with the right trappings, this is not epic stuff intended to break new ground, but it's clean, it's crisp and it delivers the goods.

Other equally compelling adventures of Ruffin T Justice include *Valley of the Golden Tombs* with Justice manufacturing a sentence in a hell-hole jail in order to break-out a psychopathic bandit and make their escape across the Mexican border. *Widow Creek* and *The Riverboat Queen* both utilised the unusual setting of a steam-boat, with the latter superior in my view due to its use of a pirate, which must be some kind of first for a western. *Dark Angel Rising* had a simple plot, with Justice forming an uneasy alliance with a sadistic gang, but the vivid characterisation and underground caverns hosting the climax mark this out as different to the herd.

Based on the Justice books I've read, author Lederer was evidently his own harshest critic, and he should know that he never short-changed a reader with these gritty, lean and inventive books.

The Ruff Justice series

1. Sudden Thunder,1981
2. Night of the Apache,1981
3. Blood on the Moon, 1981
4. Widow Creek, 1982
5. Valley of the Golden Tombs,1982
6. Spirit Woman War,1982
7. Dark Angel Riding, 1982
8. The Death of Iron Horse, 1983
9. Wind-Wolf, 1983
10. Shoshone Run, 1983
11. Comanche Peak, 1983
12. Petticoat Express,1984
13. Powder Lode, 1984
14. The Stone Warriors,1984
16. High Vengeance, 1984
17. Drum Roll, 1984
18. Riverboat Queen, 1985
19. Frenchman's Pass,1985
20. The Sonora Badman, 1985
21. The Denver Duchess, 1985
22. The Opium Queen, 1985
23. The Death Hunters, 1985
24. Flame River,1986
25. Jack of Diamonds, 1986
26. Twisted Arrow, 1986
27. The Thunder Riders, 1986
28. The Lady Was an Outlaw, 1986

FROM THE SAN DIEGO UNION-TRIBUNE

Paul Joseph Lederer, the La Mesa author of more than 100 novels, many of them Westerns, has died. His children said he suffered a brain aneurysm over the weekend.

Born in Ocean Beach, Lederer attended San Diego State and was in Air Force intelligence during the Vietnam War. He got into writing more out of necessity than passion, he said in a Union-Tribune interview last August, when he was 70.

"I was up one morning on the Black Sea, in Turkey, and I looked out over the ocean and I said, 'OK, you've got to do something, boy.'

"Once I had an artist praise my work, and once I had a writing teacher in high school who said, 'That's pretty good,' so I thought, OK, it's one of the two. Either that or manual labor, and I don't like that much, although I ended up doing a lot of that. I thought writing was something I could do and make a decent living."

Lederer was probably best known for his Indian Heritage Series. There were eight books, each about 500 pages, published in the 1980s. He did one on Tecumseh and his agent told him "Indian stories are in" so he did more: "Manitou's Daughter," "Way of the Wind," "North Star" and so on.

Cimarron Star, set on the Kansas frontier at the start of the Civil War, took him about 10 years to write. Others he did in about six weeks, cranking them out to meet a demand in the 1980s for Westerns. None of them started with an outline.

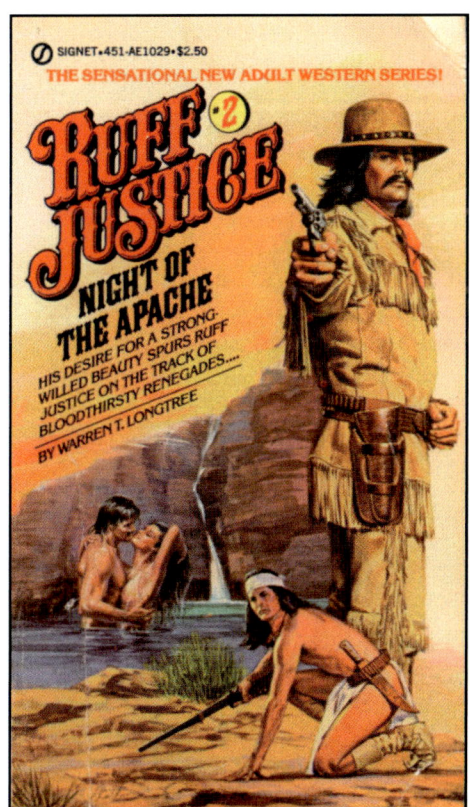
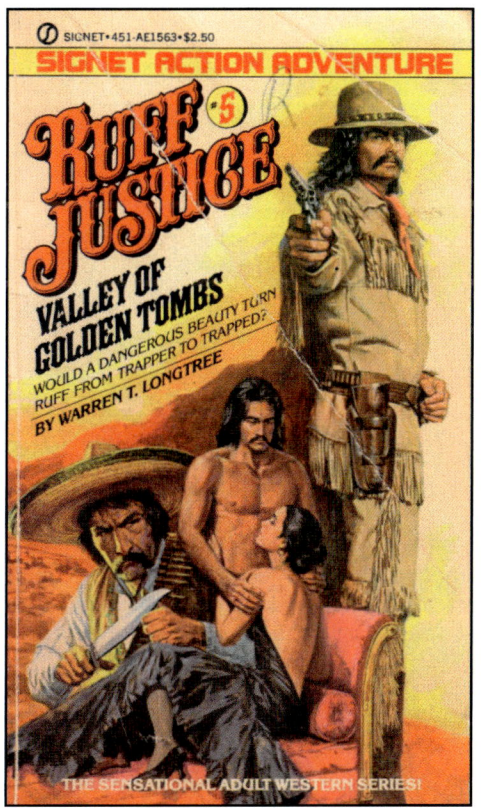

DRAW! A TOP TEN OF COMIC BOOK WESTERNS

FEATURE BY IAN MILLSTED

ACCEPTING THE ROLE OF THE LONE GUNMAN I PRESENT HERE MY COMPLETELY ARBITRARY AND SUBJECTIVE LIST OF THE BEST COMIC BOOK WESTERNS EVER. I DOUBT EVERYONE, OR EVEN ANYONE, WILL AGREE WITH MY CHOICES. INDEED, I WELCOME DISAGREEMENT. LET'S GET SOME DISCUSSION GOING HERE. WRITE IN TO THE EDITORIAL ADDRESS WITH YOUR CASE FOR THE SERIES I'VE OMITTED. MY CHOICES ARE GIVEN IN REVERSE ORDER WITH A LIST OF HONOURABLE MENTIONS AT THE END.

10. Caleb Hammer

Or more accurately "The Coming of Caleb Hammer" which was a single issue appearance in Marvel Premiere 54 (June 1980). Several years after the last new western comics from Marvel (although they had been publishing reprints until a year or so earlier) this was a brave move by the publisher at a time when the western was considered dead. The choice was made to latch onto what public recognition lingered for the genre with the physical look of the character resembling more than a little the title character in Clint Eastwood's 'The Outlaw Josey Wales'. With a cover by emerging star artist Frank Miller, a script by Peter Gillis and internal art from Gene Day and Tony Dezuniga, Caleb Hammer was the story of a Pinkerton detective with a troubled past. It hasn't dated and still reads well. Back issues are relatively easy to come by at lowish prices. A few years ago I interviewed Peter Gillis who said that there had been talk of the character continuing in one of Marvel's larger black and white magazines with art by John Buscema but sadly that never happened. Even more sadly, highly talented Canadian artist died in 1982 at the young age of 31. Caleb Hammer eventually returned but that is a story for another entry below.

9. Rawhide Kid

Marvel Comics liked western characters to have the word 'kid' in there somewhere. They were pretty hokey, very wholesome (the heroes only ever shot the guns out the bad guts hands) and often great fun. There had been an earlier comic with this title in the 1950s but my pick is the version that ran from 1960. Johnny Bart was the Rawhide Kid; fast with a gun but a loner and wanted by the law. As created by writer Stan Lee and artist Jack Kirby, the Kid owed a little to Audie Murphy's early western movies. The main concept was nothing original. The Rawhide Kid was a wandering cowboy who found himself in a new adventure each issue. What gave it a lasting appeal was the simple, direct storytelling which applied the Marvel super-hero style to a western comic. Once Stan Lee's brother, Larry Lieber, took over as both writer and artist from 1964 the series developed a sense of pathos alongside the action. Like Peter Parker (Spider-Man), Rawhide Kid always tried to do the right thing but never got any recognition for it. The run of new stories stopped in 1973 but reprints were published until 1979. The character has been revived for two limited series in the 21st century in which the Kid has been re-written as a gay character albeit never much more than being a bit camp.

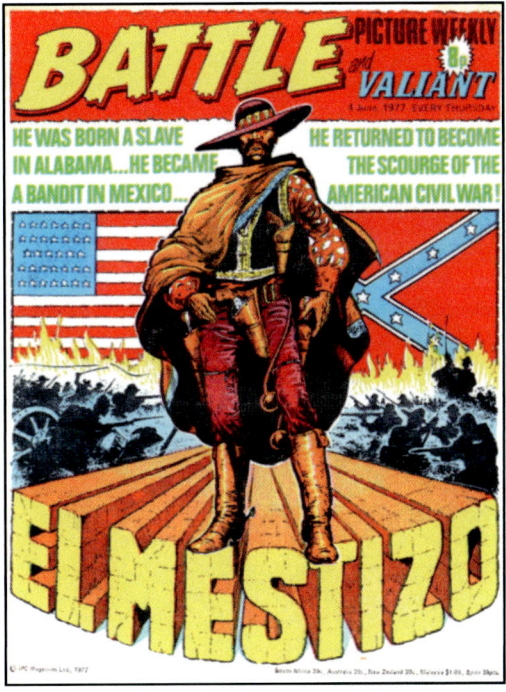

This was an unashamed attempt to do a spaghetti western in a comic aimed at 8 to 12 year old boys

---

8. El Mestizo

If ever there was an artist born to draw westerns it is Carlos Ezquerra, although this is about the only one he has done. Written by Alan Hebden, 'El Mestizo' was a series in Battle comic in 1977. This was contemporary to the launch of 2000A.D. for which Ezquerra drew 'Judge Dredd' and it is the latter which has dominated his career. 'El Mestizo' snuck into Battle due to it's American Civil War setting but I doubt anyone was fooled. This was an unashamed attempt to do a spaghetti western in a comic aimed at 8 to 12 year old boys. The fact that it didn't run long suggests the lads of the day preferred 'D-Day Dawson'. Shame really, but if you want to find out more the look for the reasonably priced hardback collection.

7. Desperadoes

'Desperadoes' is a weird-western comic that first appeared in 1997 by writer Jeff Mariotte and artist John Cassaday at a time when the only way to get a western published was to incorporate supernatural horror elements (see also the Jonah Hex and Lone Ranger comics from around the same time). However, 'Desperadoes' had an original feel to it and an interesting cast of characters which steered away from the usual white male protagonist. Cassaday's art was excellent – to the extent that he was recruited for higher profile, and better paying, comics. His replacements on subsequent series were fine but didn't quite hit the same high water mark. Most of the stories are still available in collected editions.

6. Riders of the Range

Pub question for you: "What links a popular television singer and the Eagle comic of the 1950s?".

Okay, the answer is obviously this series. 'Riders of the Range' started out as a radio series with a young Val Doonican as part of the support singing group, 'The Four Ramblers'. The radio show ran on the BBC from 1949 to 1953 but the comic version was longer lasting as a regular in the Eagle from 1950 to 1962. The writer of both versions was Charles Chilton, who also wrote the radio science fiction series 'Journey Into Space'. The main artist was Frank Humphries. 'Riders of the Range' was, at its best, well-researched and exciting. Both Chilton and Humphris were fans of the genre. For most of the time the series was running there were also annuals released for the Christmas market.

5. Lucky Luke

I don't know if anyone ever tried using the answer 'Morris' to the question "can you name five famous Belgians?" but it should definitely count. Morris, real name Maurice De Bevere, was the artist of the Lucky Luke series of graphic albums that have been published continuously since 1946. Lucky Luke can be laugh-out-loud funny and the cast of characters are cartoon classics. Morris died in 2001 but the series continued by other hands. There have been cartoon and live action films but the comics are the real thing.

4. Matt Marriott

'Matt Marriott' was a newspaper comic strip in the London Evening News from 1955 to 1977. The scripts by Jim Edgar were mature, in the proper sense of the word, and the art by Tony Weare was some of the best regular western comic art there has been. Weare could draw horses, stagecoaches, rifles and all the rest of the images expected of a story set in the American West. It always looked real. When Weare died in 1994 his obituaries suggested that Prince Philip had been a fan of the series. Why not? Sadly the series remains largely unrecognised in the U.K. While there are collections of the series available in Italy, there have been no commercial book collections in Britain. It's about time someone changed that.

---

3. Blaze of Glory

This was a four-issue series from Marvel Comics in the year 2000 in which most of their western characters were combined in a single narrative. It shouldn't really have worked but it does. The conceit is that the versions of Rawhide Kid, Two Gun Kid, Kid Colt, Ghost Rider and the rest that readers are familiar with are pulp comic versions of the actual people. Writer John Ostrander is teamed up with the excellent artist Leonardo Manco. It probably does help to have some familiarity with the characters beforehand but the story is a satisfying one. A sequel, 'Apache Skies', followed in 2002.

Hex is an ugly anti-hero that reflected the same sensibilities shown in the western novels by the likes of George G. Gilman (Terry Harknett) that were popular at the same time as the first series was running.

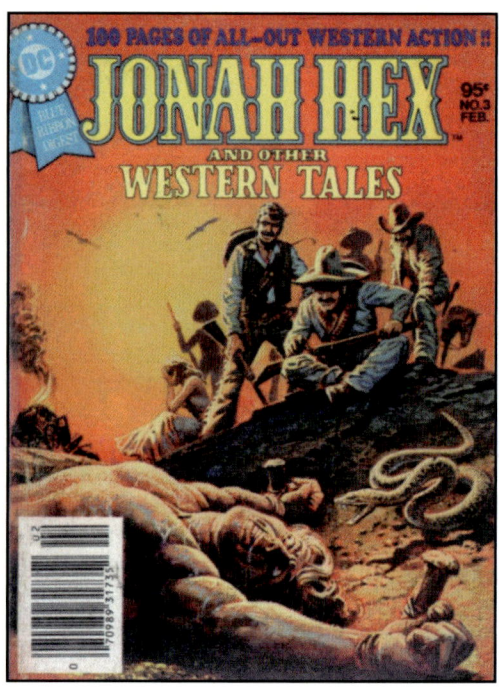

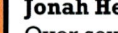 **Jonah Hex**

Over several decades 'Jonah Hex' has bucked the trend by being a long lasting success when just about no other western comic was being published in the U.S. Having first appeared in 1972, by the time the first series finished in 1985 he had been the last man standing among western characters for a number of years. (We won't talk about the science fiction version of the character that followed). There were three weird western version serials in the 1990s by the great team of Joe R. Lansdale and Tim Truman. Jonah Hex returned in a continuous series from 2006 to 2011, followed by further issues in a new title for a year or so after that. There was a not very good film and the character has appeared in the TV series 'Legends of Tomorrow'. Hex is an ugly anti-hero that reflected the same sensibilities shown in the western novels by the likes of George G. Gilman (Terry Harknett) that were popular at the same time as the first series was running. Many hands have produced the comics over the years and something about the character has brought out career best work from the likes of writer Michael Fleischer and artist Dick Ayers.

Pause for dramatic tension....

My list of honourable mentions will inevitably miss noteworthy comics. From DC Comics also worth looking at are both short runs of 'Bat Lash', the Scalphunter series from Weird Western Comics, the family saga 'The Kents' and the mature readers series 'Loveless'. Marvel also scored with 'Two Gun Kid', 'Gunhawks' and 'Red Wolf'. Three publishers have achieved success with their version of 'The Lone Ranger'. The British comic 'Look In' included an excellent adaptation of the western television series 'Kung Fu'. I could go on, but my nomination for top western comic series goes to...

The adventures of Mike Blueberry, have ranged across all the vistas of the old west; the cavalry fort, Indian wars, small town sheriffs, railroads, buffalo hunts....

1. **Blueberry**
Starting in 1963, the adventures of Mike Blueberry, have ranged across all the vistas of the old west; the cavalry fort, Indian wars, small town sheriffs, railroads, buffalo hunts, etc. The creation of writer Jean-Michel Charlier and artists Jean Giraud (aka Moebius), Blueberry rose from what was intended to be an ensemble cast to become the star of the series. There have been variations on the title (Young Blueberry, Marshal Blueberry, Fort Navajo) and other creators involved, including New Zealander Colin Wilson, but the character and series combine to make up a fine body of work. Sadly this is another series which is not fully available in English and some of the earlier volumes that have been translated are long out of print and very pricey if found second-hand. The series benefits from reading in order where possible. Enjoy.

OTHER VINTAGE PAPERBACK RELATED PUBLICATIONS FROM THE HOT LEAD TEAM

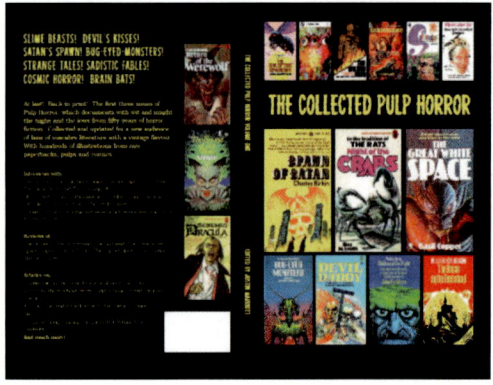
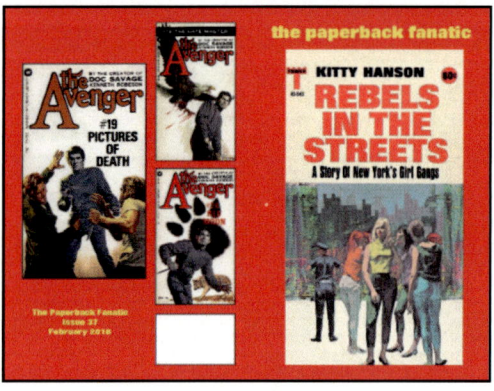

GIT YOURS TODAY! ALL AVAILABLE THROUGH AMAZON

Made in the USA
Monee, IL
15 February 2020